HEALTH AND SOCIAL CARE

Preparing to work in
adult social
care

LEVEL 2

Clare Cape
Mark Walsh
Pat Ayling
Janet McAleavy

Nelson Thornes

Please note that OCR has only endorsed the content relevant to its Preparing to Work in Adult Social Care qualification specifications

Published in 2012 by:
Nelson Thornes Ltd
Delta Place
27 Bath Road
CHELTENHAM
GL53 7TH
United Kingdom

12 13 14 15 16 / 10 9 8 7 6 5 4 3 2 1

A catalogue record for this book is available from the British Library

ISBN 978 1 4085 1812 0

Cover photograph: Douglas Forbes

Illustrations by Katherine Baxendale and Angela Knowles

Page make-up by GreenGate Publishing Services, Tonbridge, Kent

Printed and bound in Spain by Graphycems

Acknowledgements
ppiv, v Reed Social Care; p1 Monkey Business/Fotolia; p3 Gina Sanders/Fotolia; p6 goodluz/Fotolia; p10 mocker_bat/Fotolia; p16 Nicole S Young/iStockphoto; p33 Ocskay Bence/Fotolia; p39 Alexander Raths/Fotolia; p47 Fred Froese/iStockphoto; p48 Yuri Arcurs/Fotolia; p50 MarkCoffeyPhoto/iStockphoto; p51 Monkey Business/ Fotolia; p55 Alexander Raths/Fotolia; p56 delihayat/ iStockphoto; p58 auremar/Fotolia; p65 WoodyStock/ Alamy; p70 LeggNet/iStockphoto; p72 Paul Doyle/Alamy; p75 Minerva Studio/Fotolia; p76 azndc/iStockphoto; p81 Rich Legg/iStockphoto; p84 detailblick/Fotolia; p88 Paul Doyle/Alamy; p91 Odua Images/Fotolia; p93 fstop123/iStockphoto; p97 pixdeluxe/iStockphoto; p99 Beau Lark/Corbis; p123 bowdenimages/iStockphoto; p128 ImmortalBliss/iStockphoto; p139 Kallista Images/CDC/ Getty; p161 RGtimeline/Fotolia; p164 stokkete/Fotolia; p165 David Taylor/Alamy; p171 Engine Images/Fotolia; p174 Stephen Coburn/Fotolia; p175 Lisa F. Young/Fotolia.

Reed Social Care would like to acknowledge the following contributors:
• Circle
• Coventry City Council
• Places for People.

We would like to acknowledge the following contributors from within Reed Social Care:

Niall Morgan, Leslie Weare, Gladys Wright, Helen Clark, Jason Paterson, Rav Grewal, Catherine Maskell, Chris Quy.

Contents

Introduction

Reed Social Care and Community Care

Reed Social Care is the UK's leading recruitment consultancy for high-quality, dedicated social care staff. From a nationwide network of offices, we find work for qualified and unqualified social workers, community support and residential work professionals, throughout the public and private sectors. For those people who come to work for Reed, we offer industry-leading training and support, to enable people to progress their careers.

Reed Community Care provides support and carers directly to those in the community. We run extensive training courses, and offer support throughout, in order to provide the best possible care to the people we work with.

Entering the adult social care job market

The social care job market is a challenging one to enter at the present time, particularly in the public sector where budget cuts mean that organisations are seeking to employ only the highest-quality staff that they can find. Managers are looking for professional, conscientious employees who really want to work in the social care sector, and who display commitment and enthusiasm for supporting the people that they care for on a daily basis.

However, an ageing population also means increased demand for high-quality care staff – something that will continue for the foreseeable future as a greater proportion of the population requires support and care. With the right help and application, you really could find yourself in a job for life.

The purpose of this book is to help you to complete your Level 2 Preparing to Work in Adult Social Care qualification and to gain your certificate. It also aims to help give you the tools to get a job in the adult social care sector, through work based examples and Reed employment hints and tips.

Expert help

As the leading recruitment consultancy for social care staff in the UK, Reed Social Care is ideally placed to advise new workers on entering the sector, from building a CV, to finding work experience and interviewing for the ideal job for you. We help hundreds of people each week to find work, in both temporary and permanent positions, and we want to share our experience with you.

That's why, throughout this book, you will find helpful hints from our highly experienced consultants, all designed to help you find that perfect job in adult social care. These tips range from advice on CV writing to interview tips and techniques, all linked in with the learning material in the book.

As well as this, Reed Social Care has gained insights from some of our biggest clients – leading recruiters within the adult social care sector – to help you understand the mindset of a potential employer. This includes the traits and skills that they would like to see in their new employees, why you need the skills taught in this book, and how they are used on a day-to-day basis within their organisations.

This is invaluable information and offers a unique insight all geared towards helping you to gain a position within adult social care.

reed.co.uk

Throughout the book, there will also be regular mention of reed.co.uk.

reed.co.uk is the UK's number 1 jobsite, featuring jobs advertised by many different employers, as well as posts advertised by Reed's consultants on behalf of their clients.

All of the positions advertised on the site are listed by sector, and are easily searchable by location, salary and type of position, to make finding a position which is right for you as easy as possible.

reed.co.uk allows you to register as an individual user and to create and download your CV online, using advice from the experts along the way. There will be regular advice throughout this book to help you to improve your CV and covering letter, and how to use them to apply for the positions which are right for you.

reed.co.uk is an ideal starting point for those looking to find a job within adult social care, and provides all the tools to enable you to improve your career prospects while learning with this book.

About this book

Welcome to your Preparing to Work in Adult Social Care Level 2 Course Book. The purpose of this book is to help you complete your Level 2 Preparing to Work in Adult Social Care Certificate. This book gives complete coverage of the qualification and includes expert employment advice from Reed Social Care to help you get a job.

This colourful text is packed full of activities to check what you have learnt and there are also exclusive tips from Reed Social Care.

The book's features include:

Unit opener – this page contains a brief introduction to each unit along with the learning outcomes you need to achieve.

 'Think about', which encourage you to think about issues in health and social care

'Find out!', which encourage you to do further research

'Did you know?', with key supporting information, such as legislation you should be aware of

Reed Social Care @work give insights from employers into which skills they value in their staff

Key Terms

'Key terms' – during your course you'll come across new words that you may not have heard before. These words are in bold in the text and the definitions have been provided.

In Practice

What would you do?

'In Practice' and 'What would you do?' – a range of real life examples of different scenarios to provide context to the topics covered. Some of them ask how you would approach the problem.

Reed Social Care tips are designed to help you get a job.

Your questions answered

'Your questions answered' – your expert authors answer some burning questions you may have as you work through the units.

'Quick Quiz' – at the end of each unit you will find ten multiple choice questions which recap what you should have learnt in the unit. Check your answers to the Quick Quiz questions with your tutor. Answers can also be found in the 'Care' section of www.planetvocational.co.uk.

Good luck!

Principles of
communication
in
adult social care settings

Everybody communicates; the ways in which people communicate make us uniquely human. Without communication you would feel lonely, isolated and unable to function as an individual or as a member of a team.

This unit discusses communication which may be verbal (words) and non-verbal (body language, gestures, touch, eye contact and pictures). Verbal and non-verbal communication methods work together, to help people make sense of what they are hearing, seeing and feeling.

This unit also discusses difficulties with communication, confidentiality and data protection. These may present particular challenges or considerations in the adult health and social care setting.

On completion of this unit you should:

- understand why communication is important in adult social care settings
- understand how to meet the communication and language needs, wishes and preferences of an individual
- understand how to reduce barriers to communication
- understand confidentiality in adult social care settings.

1.1 The importance of communication in adult social care settings

Health and social care is fundamentally about people, so effective interpersonal communication is vital in providing care services. Communication takes place:

- with people who use services in order to assess their needs and plan their care

- within teams and organisations so that information about individuals also the skills of each of your colleagues can be shared and used effectively

- with other care providers to avoid gaps and duplication in care, and to learn from their observations.

Some of the individuals may have difficulties with communication and need special assistance.

What is communication?

Communication starts with an intended message being sent ('transmitted' or 'projected') from the source. Once it reaches the destination it will have been changed because of 'noise' and the interpretation or perception of the receiver. Feedback is an essential part of the communication process and can also be affected by 'noise' (see the diagram opposite).

Senses are your body's physiological abilities that allow you to perceive the world around you. People have five senses:

- sight

- hearing

- touch

- smell

- taste.

think about

Take a few moments to consider how each of the five senses helps in receiving information from another person.

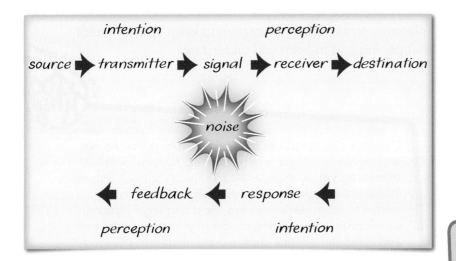

Two-way communication

You mainly use the senses of sight, hearing and touch to communicate, and occasionally the other two – smell and taste.

Remember that communication is listening (receiving) as well as talking (sending). **Effective communication** is the sharing of meaningful information between two or more people, with the goal of the receiver understanding the sender's intended message. The person who receives the message sends feedback so that the sender knows whether the message has been received and understood. The original sender of the information is responsible for recognising and understanding that feedback, and acting on it. For example, if the message wasn't understood at first, they might have to send it again, perhaps in a different way.

Why do people communicate?

Try to imagine what it would be to spend a day without communication – no conversation; no TV or radio; no reading; no computer; no phone calls or texts; no hugs. People naturally interact with each other: they benefit from and enjoy communicating. This is true whether you are an introvert (quiet and private) or extrovert (life and soul of the party).

Now try to imagine how you would do your job without communicating with individuals and your team. Can you imagine all the mistakes and repeated work that would result? Most of your job would be impossible!

Effective communication Sharing meaningful information between two or more people; the goal is that the receiver understands the sender's intended message.

Key Term

It is important to think about how you communicate

find out!

Look at an example of a multidisciplinary assessment document in use in your care setting. This provides information about the individual's problems and the actions that different members of the team are taking to meet the person's needs. There will also be sections for recording those inputs, and for reviewing or evaluating the success of those interventions in contributing to the individual's well-being, progress or recovery.

So, you can see how people communicate for work and pleasure, to make things happen, to keep up with what's happening and to learn and understand.

did you know?

Communication Studies draws on sociology, psychology, anthropology (what it is to be human), biology, political science and economics, as well as literary studies, linguistics (human language) and semiotics (signs and codes). It relates to other disciplines too, including organisational development, languages, philosophy, history, mathematics and computer science. So there are many areas in which you can learn more!

What would you do?

Mary, who has dementia, has fallen and broken her hip. She has been accompanied to hospital by a care worker from the residential care home where she lives.

1. List three things that the people involved in Mary's care need to share with hospital staff to make sure she receives the best possible support.
2. What could happen if the people involved in Mary's care don't communicate effectively with each other and with her?

How does effective communication help in the workplace?

Think about a time when something went wrong at work. Perhaps one of the team made a mistake or someone complained. It is likely that it happened because of a problem with communication. What did you and your colleagues learn from what happened?

Organisations have rules about communications that cover both **verbal communication** (such as how to answer the telephone) and written communication (such as what to include in letters sent by the organisation). These rules will be described in policies, guidelines and standards. Make sure that you are familiar with

Verbal communication When a message is delivered by being spoken.

Key Term

them. Following the rules ensures that everyone keeps to the law and shows a professional and reliable image to the public.

Most organisations seek and use feedback from the people who use their services. As a team member this may mean asking questions like 'Was everything OK for you today?' or 'Is there anything else I can do for you?'

Sometimes a letter from an individual – either giving praise or complaining – can be useful for exploring what works well and what could be improved.

Health and social care organisations may use surveys and support groups to obtain feedback.

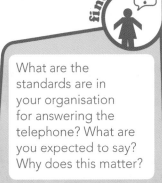

What are the standards are in your organisation for answering the telephone? What are you expected to say? Why does this matter?

Communication/feedback – Coventry CC

Customer feedback informs development of social care from front line delivery to inspection standards. It is all about the journey of the individual and the quality of service they have received. Staff as well as organisations need to reflect on customer feedback to ensure they use this information to evaluate and design their delivery and training.

Coventry City Council

@work

What can you learn by watching how people communicate?

You need to watch the person you are communicating with in order to find out whether they have understood what is going on. They might reply by speaking to you but you also need to look at their body language and facial expressions.

Some colleagues may be particularly skilled at having 'sensitive' conversations with individuals. These skills need to be learnt and may include developing empathy with the person, or stepping 'into their shoes', by using similar language, gestures and possibly touch. Spend some time with experienced colleagues to observe these skills.

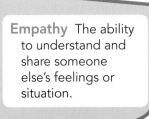

Empathy The ability to understand and share someone else's feelings or situation.

Key Term

1.2 Meeting the communication and language needs, wishes and preferences of an individual

Some people like to work things out for themselves. They may look at a map rather than ask directions.

Everyone has their own preferred ways of communicating and their own particular language needs. Think about how you like to communicate:

- Do you prefer to talk or text?
- Do you prefer to book a holiday at a travel agent or online?
- If you are lost, do you prefer to be given directions or look at a map?
- What languages are spoken in your area?
- What languages do you speak?

At the first contact with an individual, you should assess their needs and preferences for communication and agree how this will be done.

Some people may need you to adapt your approach to meet their specific needs. For example, you may need to organise support such as arranging for a translation into another language, or signing.

People from different backgrounds and traditions are likely to use some different verbal expressions and gestures, for example, for greetings and in paying respect. By showing that you understand these, you are likely to be able to build a positive relationship with the person.

People who may need particular arrangements include anyone:

- who does not speak English as their first language
- with hearing difficulties
- with sight loss
- with learning difficulties

Dementia A condition affecting the brain. People with dementia often have memory problems and there may be changes in the way the person experiences their surroundings; they will need extra support with communication.

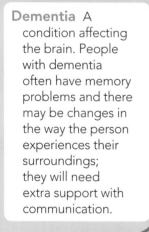

Key Term

with emotional challenges or distractions, or mental health problems

with memory loss, including dementia.

Communication and language needs of individuals

Everyone is different; so you need to understand the preferences of those using your services and try to use their preferred methods of communication. Communicating in different ways makes it easier for people to understand the message you are trying to get across. People tend to have a preference for either hearing or seeing information; although a combination often works best of all. For example, consider the following.

If you describe the directions to a place while showing the route on a map, the person is less likely to get lost. This is because you are communicating in a way that meets both hearing and seeing preferences.

Many people are not confident readers. Did you know that the average reading age in the UK is about that of a seven year old? So use short sentences and straightforward expressions for written communication, supported by pictures or diagrams.

Many people speak English as a second language, and some individuals may have very limited English. Maybe English is a second language for you or a colleague.

Communication methods

Maybe you have had the opportunity in the classroom to consider some of the ways in which people communicate, for example:

talking and listening – face to face, group lectures and debate

writing and reading – emails, leaflets, plans, records

gestures, facial expressions, body language

diagrams, pictures, charts, maps

Braille, sign language and Makaton

find out!

What is the policy in your organisation for providing translation services for individuals? How do you access this service?

Braille A system widely used by blind people to read and write. Each character consists of up to six raised dots arranged in a rectangle.

Sign language Uses visual sign patterns to convey meaning by combining hand shapes, and movement of the hands, arms or body, and facial expressions. British Sign Language (BSL) is the preferred sign language in the UK.

Makaton A system of signs and symbols to help communication. It supports the spoken word by using the signs and symbols in spoken word order.

Key Term

think about …?

media – TV, websites, newspapers

telephone and texts

feedback – questionnaires, surveys.

Communication is an essential skill for those in leadership roles. There are times when a leader will simply tell you what to do, for instance if there is an urgent situation. At other times leaders may need to coach you in order to get you to 'buy in' to a change; or will delegate responsibility for a task.

Your questions answered

When should I seek advice about communication?

Make sure you know about the various communication methods used by your team. For example:

Standards for care records – completed at the time care was provided; accurate and complete; containing fact, not opinion.

Using technology – find out what to do if the computer or phone system is temporarily unavailable.

If you are away from your workplace and have personal information with you – find out what you should do to keep it safe.

If things go wrong – make sure you know who to contact for advice, and how to report incidents and complaints.

Sometimes people over-react to bad news or frustrating circumstances. Many organisations have a 'zero tolerance' policy regarding physical or verbal violence. Report any instances to your manager, who will provide advice and support. You will also have the chance to learn how to calm situations down through working with and observing experienced colleagues.

Pick one or two activities from the list below that you've not tried before and have a go!

Read a poem or listen to a piece of music with a friend, then debate the writer's mood.

Talk with your manager or the organisation's complaints department to learn how complaints are dealt with and used for improvement.

Make notes about how using a shared diary for your team could ease communication – and then try sharing your work diary with your colleagues.

If you are a 'texter', talk on the phone instead for a day and reflect on what you learnt.

Play a game of 'charades' with your friends or family and notice who finds it easiest / most difficult. Why might that be?

As a health and social care worker you are a leader some of the time. Find a convenient time to talk with your manager or mentor about your ideas for how you could communicate in a leadership role.

1.3 Reducing barriers to communication

Discuss the following statement with a colleague: 'If it's not written down it didn't happen.'

What are the barriers to communication?

Reflect on the times you have found communication difficult and why this happened. You may find it useful to discuss this with a colleague.

1. Were there loud sounds around you, such as music, conversation or machinery?

2. Did the person have difficulty reading?

3. Was one of you thinking about something else or in a hurry?

4. If the subject was technical, was one person using words that the other person couldn't understand?

5. Did one person have difficulty in speaking or hearing?

Barriers to communication are distractions or 'noise' that interfere with sending and receiving a message. Review the diagram of two-way communication on page 2 of this unit.

There are four types of noise or distraction:

- physical or external noise – distractions in the environment such as cold rooms, unusual sounds and sights

- physiological noise – biological factors such as anxiety, feeling unwell, in pain, tired or hungry, a person's disabilities, and the effects of alcohol or drugs

- psychological noise – preconceptions and assumptions, such as a lack of confidence or believing that someone from a different country cannot speak English well

- semantic noise – using words that are confusing such as jargon, technical expressions and abbreviations.

Find out what speech, language and advocacy services are available for people using your organisation's services.

What leaflets about your services are provided in other languages and Braille?

How does your organisation communicate with its clients who use sign language?

Research some charities and organisations that can support people in your setting, such as the Stroke Association and the Royal National Insitute for Deaf People (RNID).

When you communicate with an individual you should notice how the person responds to your message. Remember that you can pick up signals from their body language as well as how they reply to you. It is important to do this so that you know the person has perceived your message in the way you intended it, and that they have understood what you have said. If an individual perceives or interprets your message differently to what you intended, they may not take the actions that you are expecting. This is turn could affect the successful outcome of the care. If necessary you could repeat the information in a different way to overcome the barrier that has led to the misunderstanding. Particularly relevant examples of this is for health promotion such as quitting smoking, or where the person is managing a long-term condition and needs to take medication correctly. Remember to consider how your reactions could be perceived by the other person.

Key Term

Stroke A stroke is caused by a blockage in a blood vessel or a bleed into the brain. This damages part of the brain and the function associated with that part. Strokes affect people in different ways, depending on the part of the brain that is affected and the extent of the damage. Recovery from a stroke depends partly on the speed at which the condition is recognised and first treatment is given.

In Practice

Beechvale House is a community social care setting. It provides a number of services, including:

- English language classes for asylum seekers who originate from non-English speaking countries

- a drop-in centre for children with moderate learning difficulties

- a luncheon club service for older people and people with sensory impairments and physical disabilities

- self-help groups for people who have had a **stroke** or have dementia or mental health problems.

The staff at Beechvale House are very busy. They have little time to sit with the individuals and build relationships.

Suggest five barriers to communication that people might experience at Beechvale House and say how you would help overcome them.

How can you reduce and overcome barriers to communication?

Go back through the list of times when you may have found communication difficult and think about how to deal with these.

Here are some ideas:

1. Always check the other person's understanding of the information you have given them by asking questions or encouraging them to repeat what you have told them. If this is difficult for them to do, think about how else they can show they have understood. Getting this feedback will help you to communicate in a different way if you need to.

2. If the environment is noisy, move away from the noise or close the window; ask if you can turn off the TV.

3. If there are reading difficulties, you'll need to recognise this and assess the person's literacy. Offer help in filling out forms and explain written information.

4. Consider using technical aids such as computer software, or human aids such as translators or interpreters.

5. If the person is finding it difficult to concentrate, ask if there is a better time to have the conversation. If it is important to have the conversation now, keep it brief and straightforward; check that the other person has understood what you have said and encourage them to ask questions.

6. Avoid jargon and **acronyms**; provide enough explanation about a technical subject for the other person to understand; consider using some written information with diagrams. Replace acronyms by using the words in full if you can.

7. For people with reading difficulties, consider describing medication by its colour and shape rather than by name.

8. If someone is distracted, back up what you have said in writing and explain how to follow it up.

think about

Make sure that you understand the other person's use of verbal expressions and gestures and that they are not misunderstanding yours. Even if the other person speaks good English, remember that cultural differences and context may affect your understanding of their response.

Make sure that you can explain how an individual from a different culture, represented in your local community, greets a family member and another person in a professional capacity, and how they indicate 'yes' and 'no'.

Paying respect and negotiation are other areas where there may be important cultural differences. By understanding these, and using them as appropriate, you are more likely to have a successful interaction.

Acronym A word formed by the first letters of other words, for example GP (general practitioner).

Key Term

1.4 Confidentiality in adult social care settings

What is confidentiality?

Typically, communication between a person and a professional such as a doctor or lawyer is private or 'privileged', and may not be discussed or passed on to others. The 'need to know' principle underpins confidentiality and information security. In adult health and social care settings, individuals' records are considered to be confidential. Records should be kept securely and only shared within the team or with another professional where that person needs to know that information, for example, where that knowledge is essential to providing care. Before passing on any confidential information, ask yourself, 'Does this person really need to know this?'

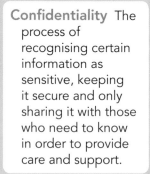

Confidentiality The process of recognising certain information as sensitive, keeping it secure and only sharing it with those who need to know in order to provide care and support.

Key Term

How does confidentiality affect people in the workplace?

Health and social care organisations have rules about handling personal information, whether it is written or spoken. This is known as information governance. You must make sure that you are familiar with the policies and guidelines in your organisation and department.

Here are some practical tips that describe how to maintain confidentiality in your day-to-day communication within your work setting:

- Make sure that you know who you are speaking with on the phone.

- Keep written information about individuals secure, for instance in a locked cabinet.

- Make sure that you understand and keep to the rules in your work-place about keeping electronic communication about individuals safe.

The Data Protection Act (1998) protects people's rights to keep their personal data (that is, information about them) private. Anyone holding personal data about living people in the UK must normally comply with the Act.

● Never discuss individuals outside your work, even without using their name. If you need to talk about your work with a colleague away from the workplace, make sure that you cannot be overheard.

● Individuals have a right to privacy, so make sure you gain their consent if you need to discuss their circumstances or care with family members.

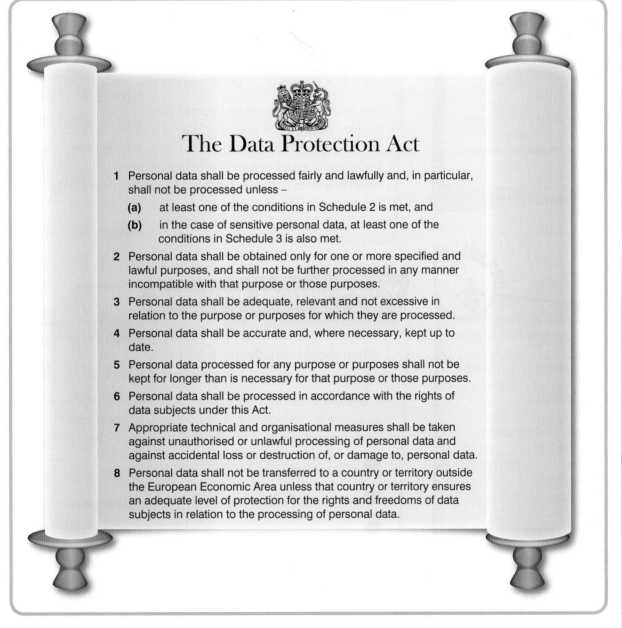

The Data Protection Act

1 Personal data shall be processed fairly and lawfully and, in particular, shall not be processed unless –

   (a) at least one of the conditions in Schedule 2 is met, and

   (b) in the case of sensitive personal data, at least one of the conditions in Schedule 3 is also met.

2 Personal data shall be obtained only for one or more specified and lawful purposes, and shall not be further processed in any manner incompatible with that purpose or those purposes.

3 Personal data shall be adequate, relevant and not excessive in relation to the purpose or purposes for which they are processed.

4 Personal data shall be accurate and, where necessary, kept up to date.

5 Personal data processed for any purpose or purposes shall not be kept for longer than is necessary for that purpose or those purposes.

6 Personal data shall be processed in accordance with the rights of data subjects under this Act.

7 Appropriate technical and organisational measures shall be taken against unauthorised or unlawful processing of personal data and against accidental loss or destruction of, or damage to, personal data.

8 Personal data shall not be transferred to a country or territory outside the European Economic Area unless that country or territory ensures an adequate level of protection for the rights and freedoms of data subjects in relation to the processing of personal data.

The Data Protection Act has eight principles for protecting information

think about

Your own and colleagues' personal information will be held confidentially by the Human Resources department. You must not share a colleague's personal information with anyone else without their permission.

Explain what you would do if you were asked for a team member's personal phone number?

Your questions answered

How and when should I seek advice regarding confidentiality?

There will be times when you need to seek advice and support about how to maintain confidentiality in health and social care work settings. For example, you may be asked for information by others in authority such as the police, other government agencies or the person's GP. There are also occasions where you may need to proactively pass on information, such as to warn of a hazard or to protect someone from harm.

You should ask advice as soon as possible from a senior colleague or your manager if you are asked to, or think you should, share confidential information. You should avoid discussing your concerns with anyone else in order to protect the confidentiality of the person's information.

find out!

Health and social care settings often have to communicate with other organisations such as care homes, voluntary organisations, hospitals and doctors. Make sure you understand what information you are expected to share, and with whom you should share it.

Your questions answered

When should confidential information be shared?

There are important exceptions to confidentiality, such as where it conflicts with the duty to warn of a hazard or to protect clients from harm. Examples include:

- suicidal behaviour
- statements indicating plans to kill another person
- abuse of children and vulnerable adults.

If the practitioner or clinician has reasonable suspicion, they are responsible for warning intended victims, and will be protected from prosecution.

Quick Quiz

1 Which three senses do you mainly use to communicate?
   a. Hearing, sight and touch
   b. Touch, smell and taste
   c. Smell, hearing and taste
   d. Taste, hearing and touch

2 Which of the following is not an example of 'the media'?
   a. Television
   b. Website
   c. An advertisement
   d. A bank account

3 Which of the following actions would you **not** use to assist communication with a person who has hearing difficulties?
   a. Speak clearly without shouting
   b. Find them a translator
   c. Ask if they prefer to use writing or symbols
   d. Face the person so that they can lip read

4 Which of the following correctly describes semantic noise?
   a. Somebody shouting at you
   b. The words you use, especially if they are complicated or full of jargon
   c. Somebody not listening to what you're saying
   d. How conversations sound to people with hearing disabilities

5 If you think somebody doesn't understand what you're saying, what should you do?
   a. Ask your manager to talk to them
   b. Repeat the information until they nod
   c. Come back later
   d. Check their understanding and then give them the information in a different way

6 What is the average reading age in the UK?
   a. 10 years   c. 4 years
   b. 7 years   d. 14 years

7 Which of the following is a justifiable reason for sharing information?
   a. The person has told you that they enjoy watching 'adult' films.
   b. The person has told you that they want to self-harm.
   c. The person has told you that they are taking part in a political demonstration.
   d. The person has told you that they are worried about being made redundant.

8 Which of the following examples describes an appropriate use of the 'need to know' principle about information?
   a. 'This information would be useful to a journalist.'
   b. 'My friend would find this interesting.'
   c. 'If my team leader knew that the client has an appointment tomorrow at the same time as their meeting, they would avoid a wasted journey.'
   d. 'If the client told me their PIN number I could get their partner to do their banking for them.'

9 Which of the following is **not** one of the key principles of data protection?
   a. Personal data shall be accurate and, where necessary, kept up to date.
   b. Personal information may be sent anywhere in the world, whenever this is necessary.
   c. Personal data shall be adequate, relevant and not excessive in relation to the purpose or purposes for which they are processed.
   d. Personal data processed for any purpose or purposes shall not be kept for longer than is necessary for that purpose or those purposes.

10 When is the best time to make a record of the care you provided?
   a. At the time of, or immediately after, providing the care
   b. At the end of your shift
   c. In response to a complaint
   d. In preparation for a court case

Principles of
personal development
in
adult social care settings

This unit will support you to understand the benefits of reflective practice. This means thinking about what you do each day in a caring environment in order to develop and improve your skills. It will also help you to apply the relevant standards when planning how to improve your skills, to look at how your personal beliefs and experiences may affect your duties and to seek guidance and feedback on how you work.

On completion of this unit you should:

● understand what is required for good practice in adult social care roles

● understand how learning activities can develop knowledge, skills and understanding

● know how a personal development plan can contribute to your own learning and development.

2.1 Requirements for good practice in adult social care roles

Good practice involves knowing why and how you perform your duties within the sector and doing your job consistently and expertly. One example is your 'duty of care'. This means that you as a carer are safeguarding the individuals who trust you to look after them and that you support their needs at all times.

This competency and knowledge comes from:

- observing, perhaps work shadowing

- reading

- listening (to individuals and to health professionals)

- asking questions and discussing (with individuals and health professionals)

- attending training courses

- being aware of the codes of practice, guidelines and legislation that govern the way you work

- agreeing to ways of working described in your terms of employment and your job description.

Tip

If you are not signed up with any recruitment agencies, now would be a good time to do so. Visit Reed.co.uk to set up an online profile and begin receiving job alerts. Reputable recruitment agencies will also be able to advise you regarding work shadowing – many organisations look for people to shadow their more experienced workers.

did you know?

Your contract of employment is a legal document. When you sign it, you are agreeing to work in the ways that your employer wants and according to national standards.

'I would like to attend a first aid course'

Standards that influence the way adult care job roles are carried out

You need to know about these important standards that make a difference to the way in which adult social care is delivered.

Codes of practice

Codes of practice are a set of behaviours that organisations agree to. They usually relate to other standards or ways of working set out by regulatory bodies. The Care Quality Commission (CQC) is the regulatory body for health and social care and uses set standards to inspect workplace performance.

National Minimum Standards

These are a comprehensive range of responsibilities related to all aspects of care. They ensure the health, safety and welfare of individuals. The minimum expected standard should be clearly evidenced in social care settings.

Essential Standards of Quality and Safety

These outline 16 aspects of care that focus on positive outcomes for individuals receiving care.

National Occupational Standards

These are a set of standards that describe skills, knowledge and understanding known as 'competencies' and they are used to inform qualifications in health and social care. They are approved by a Sector Skills Council (Skills for Care, now linked with Skills for Health). These organisations work in partnership with the CQC in regulating and promoting good care practice.

Common Induction Standards

Before you can work unsupervised you will need to understand and apply your knowledge of: the principles of caring, your role, maintaining safety, communicating effectively, recognising and responding to abuse and developing as a care worker. Ideally you learn and complete these points within six weeks.

Go to www.cqc.org. uk/standards to read more about the 16 standards of quality and safety. Browse the CQC site for more information on the other standards you need to know about.

Tip

It is essential to know about these standards for interview purposes. Ensure that you brush up on the standards before the interview, as employers will expect you to understand them.

Reflecting on work activities to develop your knowledge and skills

Reflection is a skill that enables you to think about how you work, what you do and how you relate to others: both the people in your care and the people with whom you share care duties.

Research the work of Gibbs (1998) and the 'Reflective Cycle'. This starts with thinking about a particular incident. Your awareness of what and how you did something is termed 'reflective thinking' and this often leads to improved ways of doing things.

You begin with the event and what you did at the time, then you think about it and reflect on what went well and what went less well, and so you may decide to make changes. Then something else happens and you start the cycle again. This is the process of reflection and it is how everyone learns throughout their life.

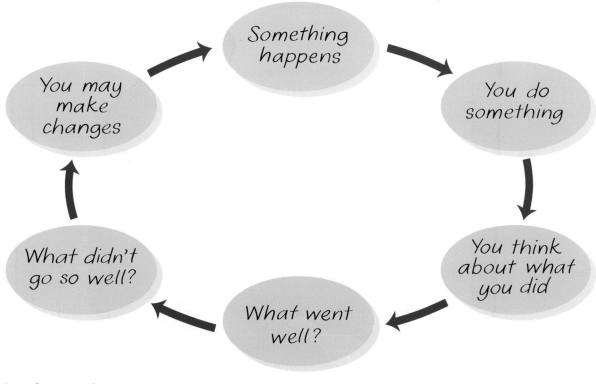

The Reflective Cycle

Mrs Salmonière is an 89-year-old French lady who has been brought to the UK to live with her daughter and son-in-law. She understands very little English and has now been placed in a residential home for respite care. She is clearly very unsettled there. She has eaten very little, refuses to drink much and is very unsteady on her feet. She has been seen rocking and weeping.

Shahina is a new care worker in the residential home.

1. How can Shahina practise good standards of care for Mrs Salmonière?

2. What will she reflect on in relation to the standards for health, welfare and safety aspects of care?

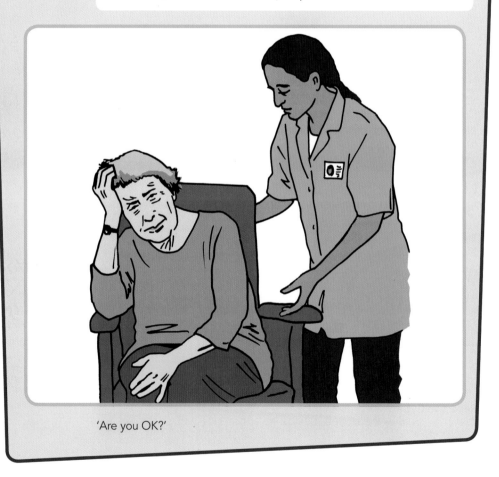

'Are you OK?'

Mrs Salmonière may present challenges that you are not used to dealing with. Some carers may respond positively to such a challenge and try to communicate with her to get information and ideas about how to settle her. Other carers will find this scary and prefer to speak in English or to leave her alone, rather than trying to discover what would help her to settle.

Ensuring that personal attitudes or beliefs do not obstruct the quality of your work

Your personal attitudes to situations in the workplace will depend on many things, for example:

- whether you feel that everyone in the UK should at least speak some English

- how you feel about other cultures – some people may not want to integrate and find it difficult to interact with people from other cultures

- how you feel about 'helplessness' displayed in the behaviour of others.

Your reactions and opinions are based on past experiences and the views of other people, usually your friends and family. For example, perhaps a carer's father often said he did not like French people as the carer was growing up.

When you work within the caring sector you will meet lots of different people. Whatever your past experiences, you must accept that everyone is different. It is a care standard to accept diversity. This includes individuals with disabilities as well as people from different cultures and speakers of other languages.

The people in your care will see you as being different from them! Imagine being taken to a hospital in a foreign country, perhaps while you are on holiday, feeling very ill and no-one speaks your language.

Thinking about how you would feel in such circumstances will enable you to have more understanding of others' situations in a care setting. That understanding will lead to empathy and you will be more likely to deliver the most appropriate high-quality care.

List four development opportunities that you think would help you to understand the needs of different individuals better. Use the list given on page 17 of this unit to help you to give examples of how you can gain this knowledge and understanding in the health and social care sector.

'What will help me to improve?'

2.2 How learning activities can develop your knowledge, skills and understanding

In the exercise at the top of this page you may have noted ways to learn such as:

- a training course for equality and diversity
- talking with your manager
- observing how senior staff respond to residents
- work shadowing
- talking to individuals in your care
- reflecting on the needs you identify and thinking about good care practice.

What would you do?

Consider the needs and preferences of two individuals.

Read about the two people below. Imagine that they are in your care and identify at least three actions from the list on page 22 that will help your knowledge, awareness and skills regarding these people.

Mrs Azarinati is unable to walk or manage her hygiene needs, following a recent stroke.

1

2

3

Mr Fleaton's vision is blurred and he easily becomes disorientated.

1

2

3

Reflecting on a situation to improve your knowledge, skills and understanding

If you do not reflect or think about what you do, your practice may never improve. It may even get worse and this would be hazardous for your colleagues as well as for the individuals you care for.

When you next attend a training course or read something useful, think about the knowledge you gain and how you can use that knowledge in the workplace. Don't forget that you are part of a team so it can also be helpful to learn from each other by talking to colleagues to share tips and experiences (without breaching confidentiality, of course).

What would you do?

Training and application of knowledge are important.

Match the training courses with the jumbled expected skills on the right.

Training	Skills that I expect to have from the training
First Aid	Keeping people safe from harm and abuse
Infection Control	Organising a 'meals from around the world' afternoon party
Equality and Diversity	Managing an unconscious person
Safeguarding	Performing a non-touch technique dressing

think about

List three health professionals who you could work shadow. Then list three experiences or activities that you would hope to gain by doing this.

Case study

In Practice

Marie is a wheelchair user in the residential home where Shahina works. Marie has been asked by the physiotherapist to do deep breathing exercises regularly, to get fresh air if possible and to keep flexing her legs to aid her circulation. She is able to take short walks.

When the physio cannot visit at the weekend, how can Shahina support Marie?

Case study

In Practice

Shahina took Mrs Harris to have a bath, but only realised the bath water was too cold when Mrs Harris had undressed. Shahina had only brought one small towel and Mrs Harris made it clear that she did not like being uncovered. She also did not have her preferred washcloth.

Shahina apologised. The next time she took someone to have a bath she made sure she had enough warm towels, that all toiletries were available and that the bath water was warm. She checked that the individual's dignity was being maintained and that choices were made before going to the bathroom.

Reflecting on her mistakes made Shahina a much better carer.

Feedback from others

Feedback is very important and should be given positively and constructively. Sometimes feedback happens spontaneously when people make comments about the service or treatment they receive.

'I always feel rushed in the morning by that carer'

'Yes, I never get my pills on time'

What would you do?

If you heard an individual make a critical comment about a service or treatment or about the side effects of their medication, what would you do?

find out !

Ask your manager for a copy of what is addressed during an appraisal meeting. List three things you think you do well and three things that you need to practise more.

It is important to report any negative comments to your line manager so that they can be addressed. You may be able to play a part in improving services and therefore contribute to your professional development as a carer.

Feedback can also be formal, such as during a supervision meeting or an appraisal.

Appraisals are two-way meetings in which you have time to prepare notes that focus on:

 what you have achieved in the setting

 what you would still like to do or any skills that you need to develop.

Some appraisals require you to seek feedback from colleagues so that all issues can be looked at in full. It is important to be honest when asking for feedback and to express your uncertainties or concerns.

You should listen carefully to constructive feedback and then reflect on how you might (or should) do things differently.

think about

How can you keep a record of your experiences, feedback and the changes you might make?

Another source of valuable feedback comes from asking the opinions of those you care for. Individuals have the right to be involved in all aspects of their care so if you ask how they feel, or if something could be done differently, you are valuing and respecting them. You will both build a trusting relationship and improve your professionalism.

Tip

REED
SOCIAL CARE

Any interviews that you attend can give you valuable knowledge and experience, even if you don't get the job. Make sure that you reflect properly on interview feedback, to learn and improve for the next interview.

2.3 How a personal development plan can contribute to learning and development

What is a personal development plan?

Setting out a personal development plan is a structured process for reflecting on and developing your skills and abilities. It involves planning for the future and you will be supported by your manager during this process.

During a supervision or appraisal meeting with your manager, you will identify some gaps in your performance. This is positive and absolutely normal, so it is important to be honest in discussing your concerns. Everyone in any job needs to keep learning and improving their skills. Observing, reading, asking questions, listening and practising new skills are all good ways to increase your knowledge and ability.

think about

Consider some skills you need to develop and how you might do this.
Copy and complete the table below.

Skill I need to develop	How might I develop this?
1 I need to learn how to shower someone using the special chair.	
2 I need to know more about the Essential Standards of Quality and Safety.	
3 I need to know how to wash someone's hair who is in bed.	
4 I need to know how to safely administer medicines.	
5 I need to know how to make a recording of a change in the care plan.	

You need to clearly identify what you want to do and make sure that your objectives include activities that you can measure. This makes it easier to work towards your goals and to know when you have reached them. When making plans for personal development, it is always important to give yourself a timescale and not put off any learning objectives.

> ## Tip
>
> REED
> SOCIAL CARE
>
> A recruitment agency can be involved in your personal development plan. Reputable agencies will contribute to a professional development fund to enable you to gain further training while you work for them. You should take your personal development plan to any interview with recruitment agencies.

Who can help you with the personal development plan process?

Talk to as many health professionals as you can about good practice.

When you identify ways to make progress in your work, ask your manager about the best way to do it. Your manager may be able to arrange some formal or informal training for you.

Formal qualifications in health and social care are usually gained at Level 2 or 3, but there are also other options such as university degrees, and the QCF Diploma involves assessments of observation in the workplace.

Some qualifications can be achieved by distance learning. This involves learning partly on the job and partly by completing some written work at home.

If you put enough time and effort into your personal development plan, you should get the results you want

Sources of support for your own learning and development

If you begin a qualification, you may attend classes with a tutor. Your tutor will support you with the knowledge aspects of the course. You will also be assigned an assessor who will assess your performance against the standards. She or he will do this by observing your performance. In addition, your manager, assessor and other health professionals form a partnership of support for your learning.

However you learn, the National Occupational Standards inform the content of your course. You must show competencies and skills in order to achieve your qualification, but your assessor will also be a source of support. Don't forget that there are additional online sources of support, such as forums where people who are also learning about health and social care can share their thoughts and questions.

Case study

In Practice

While Shahina is assisting with a medicine round at a nursing home, a woman suffers an allergic reaction to a drug.

As Shahina may one day be responsible for administering medicines, she thinks that she should be aware of what has caused the reaction and what to do.

1. Identify the resources available to Shahina to help her find out about medicines.

2. List some common medicines in use in your home and highlight a possible reaction or side effect for each.

3. Describe what Shahina should do if there is a serious side effect to a medication.

There are lots of resources online that will help you to learn more about how best to develop your career in health and social care. These include forums and online journals, as well as the websites of professional bodies. Find as many of these sources as you can and do a review by giving them marks out of 10 for information that is relevant to your job role.

Here are some examples of professional websites:

- www.dh.gov.uk (information on care standards)
- www.library.nhs.uk (information and research)
- www.open.ac.uk (Open University resources)
- www.skillsforcare.org.uk (the Sector Skills Council for care linked to the CQC, provides information on social care)
- www.skillsforhealth.org.uk (another Sector Skills Council for health care)
- www.nhs.uk/carers (NHS site with information, advice and support for carers)
- www.cqc.org.uk (Care Quality Commission)
- www.nursingtimes.net (*Nursing Times* magazine)
- www.careknowledge.com (communicating with other social care professionals)
- www.nhscareers.nhs.uk (details about careers in the NHS)
- www.hse.gov.uk (the national independent watchdog for health, safety and illness at work)
- www.ucas.ac.uk (Universities and Colleges Admissions Service manages applications to higher education courses in the UK)

The benefits of using a personal development plan

Of course increasing your skills and competencies means that you can do your job better and ensure that those you care for receive the best possible support. There are also personal benefits. For example, when you learn something new it will increase your self-esteem and, as long as you stay working in health and social care, you will want to go on improving and learning.

Progressing in your career is like going up a ladder; you climb as fast as you build your knowledge, skills and confidence.

did you know?

Many matrons in UK hospitals started as health care assistants or volunteers in the sector. They were keen to improve and did so by planning their steps to climb the ladder and gaining as much experience as they could.

REED
SOCIAL CARE
●●●

Personal development – Coventry CC

As a social care worker it is essential that you keep your personal and professional development up to date. This contributes to the safeguarding of individuals and staff by ensuring that you know about the latest developments in training and legislation. Staff need to ensure they keep their reflective journal up to date with a variety of development methods to relate theory into practice and also to support supervision and planning of development needs for the following year.

Coventry City Council

@work

It is important to keep examining your skills acquisition and competence. When you have some more experience, you will be able to make informed decisions about how you want to develop your career. There are lots of things you can do if you follow your interests and develop your strengths, for example in dementia care or community health. If you achieve a degree, you could become a nurse or a social worker. You might like to try teaching others, or to become an assessor or a manager in the sector.

Quick Quiz

1 Most of the learning in the health and social care sector is done by:
   a. reading books
   b. observing, listening, practising and reflecting
   c. doing a Level 3 course
   d. doing a degree.

2 The standards that are used to inform qualifications are:
   a. the 16 Essential Standards of Quality and Safety
   b. the Health and Safety and Fire Standards
   c. the Health and Safety at Work Regulations
   d. the National Occupational Standards.

3 Within the first six weeks of working in the health and social care sector, you should:
   a. complete your NVQ Diploma
   b. complete a recognised Food Safety Qualification
   c. complete your Common Induction Standards requirements
   d. complete your CRB and medical checks.

4 A care worker's aim is to make a difference in terms of:
   a. an individual's overall well-being
   b. the task management of a setting
   c. the fundraising of the care provision
   d. the personal care individuals receive.

5 Having prejudices against people can have significant:
   a. advantages to people's well-being
   b. negative effects on care attitudes
   c. benefits to good health
   d. benefits to diversity.

6 Negative feelings are best expressed to:
   a. your colleagues
   b. the individual you care for
   c. your manager
   d. visitors.

7 Constructive feedback on areas for development is best:
   a. ignored
   b. questioned
   c. focused on so that improvements can be made
   d. discussed with colleagues.

8 It is important to have measurable goals so that:
   a. you have something to aim for
   b. you can see the progress you've made
   c. you have evidence of what you have achieved
   d. all of the above.

9 A partnership for your learning is provided by:
   a. your family and friends
   b. your partner at home
   c. your assessor and your manager
   d. the local authority.

10 A personal development plan helps you to:
    a. reflect and target your plans for progression
    b. do the same job for as long as possible
    c. compare your progress with your colleagues
    d. manage your income.

Diversity, equality and inclusion

Modern society is made up of people from many different social and economic backgrounds, ethnic groups, countries, ages, genders, sexual orientations, abilities, religious traditions and beliefs. The culture of our society aims to promote equal opportunities for all and to be inclusive by giving everyone the chance to achieve their potential – free from discrimination and prejudice.

So it is important to think about how the terms 'equality', 'diversity' and 'inclusion' can help to improve the way you live, and the way you work in health and social care settings. This idea is embedded in law. The Equality Act came into force in October 2010, providing a single legal framework to tackle disadvantage and discrimination.

This unit introduces the concepts of equality, diversity and inclusion which are used in the Equality Act and in many policies at work. These ideas are fundamental to working in adult health and social care settings.

The unit is aimed at those who are interested in, or new to, working in social care settings with adults.

On completion of this unit you should:

- understand the importance of diversity, equality and inclusion

- know how to work in an inclusive way

- know how to access information, advice and support about diversity, equality, inclusion and discrimination.

3.1 Diversity, equality and inclusion

These terms are used throughout this unit and in the Equality Act 2010, so it is important to be clear about what they mean and their place in providing health and social care.

Diversity

Diversity is about the value of everyone's individual differences – attributes, talents and characteristics – and how these come together in a culture where everyone can take part and do well.

Your identity is the set of characteristics that define who you are. You are born with some of these characteristics, such as eye colour, race, and any genetic or congenital health problems. Other characteristics develop and may change over time, such as your personality, interests, beliefs, abilities and sexual orientation.

British history and ethnic diversity

Today, as has happened throughout history, immigrants arrive in Britain from around the world. They come for economic, political and family reasons, for example to work or because they will be more welcome here than in the countries they come from.

These are just some examples of people from elsewhere in the world arriving in Britain:

In ancient times, invasions brought people from north-west Europe, and Celtic people migrated along the west coasts of Europe. When the Romans invaded Britain, they brought with them people from North Africa.

Between the sixteenth and nineteenth centuries, African and African-Caribbean people arrived because of Britain's involvement in the slave trade. People also came from India and China because of Britain's growing Empire and its trade.

think about

In what special ways are you different from other members of your family, social group or your team at work?

How do you, or could you, use these differences to enhance each group?

In the twentieth century, wars created refugees from central Europe and beyond. Most recently, migration increased throughout the EU for economic reasons as borders were relaxed.

did you know?

Cultures are shared all over the world:
- Food – tikka masala is one of Britain's favourite dishes, and Italian pizza has been adopted as one of America's favourites.
- Music – blues and jazz are strongly influenced by the music of North Africa.
- Dance – may be influenced by traditions from around the world such as bangla, salsa and merengue.
- Sports – football's popularity has spread to many parts of the world, including South America and Africa; while Britain has imported martial arts from China and Japan.
- Fashion – is often influenced by clothing styles from Asia, India and Africa.

Equality

Equality supports the legal framework that protects against discrimination, promotes equal opportunity and supports good relations between people with '**protected characteristics**'.

Everyone has one or more of these characteristics – so everyone is protected under this law.

The core values of equality and diversity will be familiar to anyone working in health and social care and you will recognise these themes in many of the policies in your care setting:

- individual rights
- giving choices
- respect
- services in response to individual need.

These are balanced by everyone's responsibility to respect other people's rights and choices.

Protected characteristics
'Protected characteristics' in the Equality Act (2010) as it applies to users of a service are: age, disability, gender reassignment, marriage and civil partnership, pregnancy and maternity, race, religion or belief, sex and sexual orientation.

Key Term

Inclusion

By recognising and valuing the principles of equality and diversity in everyday life, people from all groups can be included in society, can feel valued and respected and able to contribute. These principles, when applied to your work in health and social care, put individuals at the centre of their care planning and support. It is important to recognise that feeling valued and respected is essential to everyone's emotional well-being.

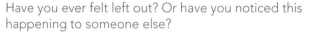

Have you ever felt left out? Or have you noticed this happening to someone else?

Did this have something to do with being of a different race, gender, sexual orientation or ability or holding different beliefs from the rest of the group?

What did you feel able to do about it?

Discrimination

Discrimination describes a situation where someone is treated less favourably than someone else because of one of the protected characteristics listed in the Equality Act. Discrimination can be direct or indirect.

Direct discrimination When a person is treated less well than someone else because of a protected characteristic (what makes them different).

Indirect discrimination When a rule or way of doing things is put in place that has a worse impact on someone with a protected characteristic (because they are different) than someone without one; and cannot be justified.

Key Terms

In Practice

Effects of discrimination

Being discriminated against may feel devastating for the person concerned, and it could damage their chances of getting the best from health or social care services.

1. What if, as a man attending an outpatient clinic, you have to have your consultation or assessment in a curtained area with less privacy, because all the private rooms have been given to women? Would you come back for your next appointment?

2. What if you are told that because you are a wheelchair user you have to be given a room on the ground floor of a residential home – even though the ground floor rooms are all smaller and darker than the ones upstairs? How might this affect your emotional well-being?

3. What if, as a gay person, you couldn't see a particular cancer specialist because of their prejudice? Might this affect your chances of recovery?

think about

Some of these examples of discrimination are direct and some are indirect. Can you identify which is which?

Individual and institutional discrimination

Discrimination by individuals is when a person acts in a way that results in someone being treated unfairly, even if anti-discrimination policies are in place.

Institutional discrimination is where the whole organisation or department works in a way that means that individuals are discriminated against. This may be because of its policies and rules or it may be the result of widely held beliefs and prejudices that affect people's behaviour and the culture of the department or organisation.

Discrimination is often a result of a lack of knowledge and understanding. This can lead to:

- prejudice – pre-judging someone's knowledge or beliefs
- labelling – for example, 'the wheelchair user' instead of Mrs Smith
- lack of opportunity – particularly in education and employment
- stereotyping – projecting beliefs about a whole community onto an individual
- harassment – unwanted and unpleasant attention or an action intended to intimidate or undermine a person
- bullying – persistant unkindness or cruelty, either physical or emotional
- use of inappropriate language – which is likely to reflect any or all of the above, for example making racist or sexist comments, or making jokes or using derogatory terms about disabilities.

Work settings

Health and social care workers are bound by the Equality Act, as it applies to individuals and employees. It is useful to be aware of which of the protected characteristics individuals may have. For example, users of health and social care services are more likely to have the protected characteristics of age or disability. Economic deprivation (lack of money) has an impact on mental and physical health and well-being, and some ethnic groups are more likely to experience certain diseases. Older people are more likely to have long-term health conditions, while a combination of conditions can make the effects worse and lead to additional need.

Some beliefs and traditions may mean that the person is less willing or able to use some parts of the health and care services on offer.

REED
SOCIAL CARE

Discrimination – a leading care home group

Discrimination in any form – whether intended or unintentional – is completely unacceptable. Often, discrimination comes from ignorance or lack of understanding, and so we encourage our employees to take the time to understand our policies, and promote the rights of our individuals and other employees at all times. Inclusion and equality are at the heart of our company culture.

Care workers must find ways of including older people and those with disabilities

@work

find out!

- Which national or religious groups are represented in your local community?
- Are there any health or social care services provided specifically to meet their needs?
- Do any of these groups hold local festivals or events? Maybe you know someone from that community and could join in?

find out!

Research the policies in your organisation.

- What would you do if you observed a colleague acting in a discriminatory way?
- What would you do if a room's layout or the available equipment seems to disadvantage some individuals?
- How would you support a patient who has offered to take part in a service development / improvement project?

Support for equality and inclusion

At the beginning of this unit you learnt about the value that differences bring. Policies and procedures in the workplace are there to ensure that the organisation acts lawfully, and that, as an employee, you have rules and guidelines to support equality and inclusion in your everyday work.

The Equality Act (2010) brought together previous anti-discrimination laws to make the law easier to understand and follow. It affects equality law at work and in delivering services. The Act protects everyone from unfair treatment because everyone has one or more of the nine protected characteristics.

The Equality Act and local policies give us the rules. However, you need to be able to take positive actions when needed.

Tip

All recruitment agencies will have policies regarding diversity and equality which they follow. You should be aware of such policies and how they affect your rights with regards to finding work through recruitment agencies.

Key Term

Dignity Having respect and status. It is generally accepted that everyone has the right to dignity and ethical treatment. Dignity is closely linked to human rights.

Your questions answered

So how does the Equality Act (2010) work in practice?

You need to develop confidence in these ideas by working with more experienced colleagues and reflecting on your practice. Think about:

- challenging discrimination – by speaking up, even though it feels risky

- promoting rights – considering the person's needs, wants and expectations

- empowering – listening and acting on the person's contribution

- removing barriers – such as physical access and timing

- communication – the way that the person needs us to give information and receive feedback

- improving participation – valuing feedback and input

- promoting dignity – treating people as you'd like to be treated

- ensuring that individuals are central to their care planning and delivery.

3.2 **Working in an inclusive way**

Human rights

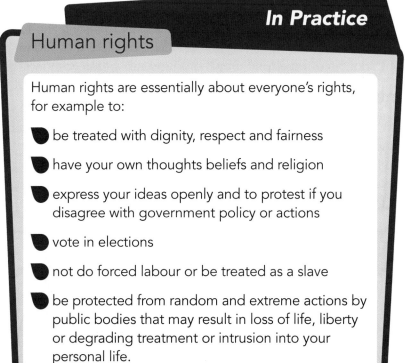

In Practice

Human rights

Human rights are essentially about everyone's rights, for example to:

- be treated with dignity, respect and fairness
- have your own thoughts beliefs and religion
- express your ideas openly and to protest if you disagree with government policy or actions
- vote in elections
- not do forced labour or be treated as a slave
- be protected from random and extreme actions by public bodies that may result in loss of life, liberty or degrading treatment or intrusion into your personal life.

All humans have similar basic needs such as for nutritious food, shelter, health care, protection from harm and education. Maslow's 'Hierarchy of needs' (see Unit 7 pages 116–17) can help you to understand the priority of these needs.

Everyone has the right to have their basic needs fulfilled. The idea of human rights supports you in all areas of your life: what you need and how you should treat others.

It is important to be clear about the difference between needs and wants. Wants are nice to have but are not essential for a person to survive and develop.

The United Nations' Universal Declaration of Human Rights

Legislation and codes of practice

The idea of human rights is expressed in the law. The purpose of the Equality Act is to protect everyone's right to be treated fairly. It does this by protecting employees at work and people using a service on the basis of the 'protected characteristics'.

Interactions and communication

In Unit 1 you saw that good communication is essential in order to work effectively with adults, children and young people, as well as with your colleagues. Barriers to communication may include distractions or 'noise', such as from your use of language or from underlying worries.

A carer assessing the needs of the person and their family

In order to be respectful, and to avoid disadvantaging people with different communication needs, you should pay attention to:

● active listening – giving verbal and non-verbal responses to the other person

- discovering and using your knowledge of the person – their beliefs, values and preferences

- maintaining confidentiality – by providing privacy and reassuring the person

- using language appropriately – and checking their and your understanding of what has been said.

Tip

Do your research prior to interview to understand the different types of individual that each organisation works with. An interview would expect you to display an understanding of the different groups and individuals that you will be working with on a daily basis, and an idea about how to deal with the different challenges that each individual represents.

Case study

In Practice

Rani, who is 79, had a stroke ten years ago. Since then she has had very limited mobility, spending all her time in bed or in a chair at home. Rani's stroke also left her unable to speak more than a few words. She and her youngest daughter Mina live in a two-bedroom flat on the second floor, with no lift. Mina is unmarried and does not work as she cares for her mother full time. The family moved to England when Mina was 12 years old and, although she speaks fluent English, it is not her first language. There are shops, a community leisure centre and a doctor's practice about half a mile away. Rani's other daughter and son-in-law live about six miles away on the other side of town and visit every few days, but Rani and Mina have very little social contact apart from this.

Rani and Mina's benefits cover rent, bills and food but there is little left for extras. Rani was widowed four years ago and both she and Mina have episodes of depression.

- Talk with a colleague about the disadvantages Mina and Rani have experienced, and whether any of these may include elements of discrimination.

- Make an outline plan for the health and social care support that you think Rani and Mina would benefit from receiving.

think about

How can you use your knowledge and experience?

If you develop a particular interest in equality, diversity and inclusion, there may be opportunities to use your enthusiasm by learning more, getting involved in reviewing and developing policies and procedures, and taking part in activities that promote inclusion of minority groups.

Challenging discrimination

Avoiding or eliminating discrimination starts with challenging your own beliefs and attitudes. The values of inclusion – individual rights, choice, respect and responsiveness – are mentioned throughout the policies and procedures of your care setting and organisation. If your own deeply held beliefs are similar to those of your organisation, you are likely to value that fit, and feel comfortable with the rules, style of working and atmosphere. You must also be aware of how your own beliefs and attitudes might affect how you work with individuals and consider how you can challenge your own prejudices to ensure they get the best care.

If you see or hear discriminatory behaviour, you should tell someone. This is not easy, so your manager may be the first person you tell. Staff who speak or act in a discriminatory way are dealt with using disciplinary procedures.

Individuals who believe they have been discriminated against may use the organisation's complaints procedures. But some people may think that, if they do this, the discrimination could become worse and so they are likely to need support and encouragement to make a complaint. It is always best to address the discriminatory behaviour as soon as possible.

> 66 When you are challenging inequality you are wearing your values on your sleeve all the time … often it was equality for myself that I was really fighting for. 99
>
> **Salma Yasmeen**

In 'Trust me I'm a health manager', NHS Institute for Innovation and Improvement, 2008

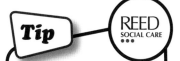

Tip

It is important to display an ability to act in an inclusive way at interview. To do so, avoid using jargon or terms which are specific to your previous employers - using terms or acronyms which your interviewer may not understand is not considered good interview practice.

did you know?

As an employee you also have the right not to be discriminated against, either by your employer or by individuals. Many health and social care organisations publish a 'zero tolerance' statement against verbal or physical abuse towards members of staff. But remember that people are likely to be displaying aggressive behaviour because they are frightened or frustrated.

Health and social care organisations are expected to provide training on equality and diversity for staff. They should do this at induction and, in some cases, every year.

3.3 Accessing information, advice and support about diversity, equality, inclusion and discrimination

Sources of information and advice

If you want to find out more, there is plenty of information available from the following organisations:

- **The Equality and Human Rights Commission** – the independent advocate for equality and human rights in Britain: www.equalityhumanrights.com

- **The National Council for Voluntary Organisations** – aims to give voice and support to civil society by acting as an umbrella organisation for the voluntary sector. Many now well-established voluntary organisations started out as projects within NCVO, including Age UK, the Citizens Advice Bureaux and Community Matters: www.ncvo-vol.org.uk

- **Age UK** – aims to improve later life for everyone by providing information, training and research: www.ageuk.org.uk

- **Stonewall** – the UK's leading lesbian, gay and bisexual charity. It carries out campaigning, lobbying and research and provides free information: www.stonewall.org.uk

- **Directgov** – the UK government's digital service for people in England and Wales. It provides information and practical advice about public services: www.direct.gov.uk

- **Skills for Health** – the Sector Skills Council for health. It helps the UK health sector develop a more skilled and flexible workforce: www.skillsforhealth.org.uk

- **Skills for Care** – ensures that England's adult social care workforce has the appropriately skilled people in the right places: www.skillsforcare.org.uk

- **Social Care Institute for Excellence** – provides e-learning resources: www.scie-socialcareonline.org.uk

- **The Nursing and Midwifery Council** – regulates nurses and midwives in the UK: www.nmc-uk.org.uk

think about

Try to pay attention to the principles of equality, diversity and inclusion in your everyday work by reflecting on how what you say and do may be perceived by others, especially by people from a minority group or with the 'protected characteristics'. It can be useful to get feedback on your work from colleagues, your manager and perhaps those in other services. You can learn more by working with community leaders or local voluntary organisations that work with specific minority groups.

Quick Quiz

1 Which of the following is **not** one of the themes or principles of human rights?
   a. To be treated with dignity, respect and fairness
   b. To voice one's ideas openly and to protest if you disagree with government policy or actions
   c. To be protected from random and extreme actions by public bodies
   d. To go to university

2 Which of the following is not one of the nine 'protected characteristics' in the Equality Act (2010) as it applies to individuals?
   a. Disability
   b. Race
   c. Being a convicted criminal
   d. Age

3 What is diversity?
   a. Equality between people
   b. Being the same as other people
   c. The value of your differences
   d. Being a different race from someone else

4 What is the main reason why you should speak up if you witness discriminatory behaviour?
   a. So that others can join in
   b. Because you must not ignore it
   c. To make the person on the receiving end aware of it
   d. To stop yourself from feeling uncomfortable about it

5 If an individual makes a complaint about discrimination, why is it best to avoid a court case?
   a. It takes a long time
   b. It can be expensive
   c. It could damage your organisation's reputation
   d. All three of these

6 What helps to support people with different communication needs?
   a. Looking away from the person while listening
   b. Discovering and using your knowledge of the person
   c. Ignoring confidentiality
   d. Using complex language and jargon

7 Which of the following statements about the Equality Act (2010) is **not** true?
   a. It does not apply to work situations.
   b. It protects everyone from unfair treatment.
   c. It made the law about equality easier to understand and follow.
   d. It brought together previous equality legislation.

8 Which of the following activities would **not** support the Equality Act (2010)?
   a. Empowering the person by listening and acting on their contribution
   b. Improving participation by using feedback
   c. Telling someone the best way to do something
   d. Promoting dignity by treating people as you'd like to be treated

9 What is the Equality and Human Rights Commission?
   a. The UK's leading lesbian, gay and bisexual charity
   b. The independent advocate for equality and human rights in Britain
   c. The Sector Skills Council for health and social care
   d. The organisation that brings together black and minority ethnic, faith, women, age and disability-related organisations

10 Which of the following is **not** a part of the set identity that you are born with and cannot change?
   a. Nationality
   b. Eye colour
   c. Skin colour
   d. A genetic condition

Principles of
safeguarding and
protection in
health and social care

This unit introduces the important area of safeguarding and protecting individuals from abuse. It identifies different types of abuse, and the signs which could indicate that abuse is occurring. It also considers when individuals might be vulnerable to abuse and what you should do if you suspect abuse. A range of factors contributes to the vulnerability of individuals who use social care services. There are some important national policies and local systems in place to protect and safeguard them. This unit focuses on the social care worker's role in this process, as well as the roles of other professionals and agencies.

On completion of this unit you should:

- know how to recognise signs of abuse
- know how to respond to suspected or alleged abuse
- understand the national and local context of safeguarding and protection from abuse
- understand ways to reduce the likelihood of abuse
- know how to recognise and report unsafe practices.

4.1 Recognising signs of abuse

What is 'abuse'?

Abuse can take many forms

Most adults can protect themselves from threats of harm – they are not **vulnerable** to abuse. However, some adults who use social care services may need **safeguarding** because they are at greater risk of, or have already experienced, abuse.

In 2000 the Department of Health published *No Secrets* which defined abuse as: 'a violation of an individual's human and civil rights by any other person or persons'.

Abuse can occur when individuals are deprived of their rights to:

- privacy
- independence
- choose for themselves
- a decent quality of life
- protection and security.

Adults in need of safeguarding can experience different types of abuse and sometimes more than one type of abuse. For example, emotionally abusive threats and intimidation often happen at the same time as physical abuse or violence. Protecting **adults at risk** of abuse is a key responsibility of every social care worker.

Key Terms

Vulnerable More likely to suffer risk and harm.

Safeguarding Ensuring the individual is safe from abuse and neglect, and helping people to make choices independently.

Adult at risk Anyone aged 18 years and over who might not be able to protect themselves because they are ill, disabled or older.

did you know?

In 2010–2011, older people reported the most incidences of abuse (61 per cent), followed by adults with a physical disability (49 per cent), clients with mental health problems (23 per cent), learning disabled clients (20 per cent) and adults experiencing substance misuse or other problems (7 per cent).

Type of abuse	Definition of abuse
Physical	Deliberate use of force that results in bodily injury or pain. Includes hitting, biting, shaking, burning, inappropriate treatments, isolation or confinement and misuse of medication.
Sexual	Involvement in sexual activity without consent. This may be direct (e.g. being forced to perform sex acts) or indirect (being forced to watch sexual activity in person or on the TV or internet). The person may not wish to **consent**, lack **capacity**, or they may feel **coerced** because the abuser is in a position of trust, power or authority.
Emotional/ psychological	Any action that damages an individual's mental well-being such as threats, humiliation, bullying, swearing or other mental cruelty that results in distress. Includes the denial of basic human rights, such as choice, self-expression, privacy and dignity.
Financial	The theft or misuse of an individual's money or personal possessions.
Institutional	Mistreatment of an individual by the authorities or people within an institution. It occurs when the routines, systems and **norms** of an institution are seen as more important than the needs of the people they support.
Self-neglect	When an individual fails to care for themselves and meet their own basic needs for food, warmth, rest, medical care and personal care. May be intentional (such as self-harm) or unintentional, due to physical or mental health issues.
Neglect by others	Failure to meet an individual's needs for personal care, food, warmth, rest, medical care, social stimulation, cultural or religious needs. This can be either acts of **omission** (not doing something) or **commission** (doing something on purpose).

Types and examples of abuse

Consent Giving informed agreement to or permission for something to happen, such as an action or decision. Establishing consent varies according to individual's assessed capacity to give consent.

Capacity The mental or physical ability to do something.

Coerce Force someone to do something against their will.

Norm Accepted, normal behaviour.

Omission Where something is either deliberately or accidentally not done.

Commission Deliberately doing something while knowing the consequences.

Key Terms

Indicators of physical abuse

Physical abuse is the easiest to recognise – you can usually see the results of it. However, it can be missed if someone makes excuses for it and some forms of physical abuse – such as denying an individual's needs or the misuse of medication – can also be more difficult to spot. If an explanation doesn't 'fit' an injury, you should always report it and ask for further investigation.

Signs and symptoms of physical abuse include:

Some signs of physical abuse can be easy to spot

- multiple or minor bruising of different areas with inconsistent explanations

- burns and scalds, including oddly shaped bruising or burns – such as the shape of an iron, weapon or cigarette end

- marks on the skin from being slapped, scratched, bitten or pinched

- broken bones or unexplained falls

- evidence of old injuries, for example untreated broken bones

- indicators of malnutrition or general signs of neglect

- misuse of medication, such as not giving pain relief or giving too much sedative

- defensive reactions by the individual when approached by anyone.

Indicators of sexual abuse

Sexual abuse can include contact or non-contact abuse:

- 'Contact' sexual abuse includes: vaginal or anal rape; touching someone or forcing someone to touch another person in a sexual way without consent.

- 'Non-contact' sexual abuse includes: indecent exposure; sexual talk, harassment or inappropriate photography; forcing a person to watch pornography or sexual activity.

Sexual abuse is often associated with the misuse of power, alongside physical and psychological abuse.

Signs and symptoms of sexual abuse include:

- fear of physical contact

- injury, bleeding, irritation or infection around the genitals

- sexually transmitted disease

- bruising, bites, scratches on the breast or inner thigh

- inappropriate conversations of a sexual nature

- unexplained crying and distress

- withdrawal from social contact

- self-harm or self-neglect.

Indicators of emotional or psychological abuse

Psychological abuse can be difficult to identify, as it is usually hidden. Sometimes those committing this kind of abuse withhold care, friendship and love, make verbal threats to frighten the individual into doing what they want, or deny them the right to make decisions.

Signs and symptoms of emotional and psychological abuse include:

- self-isolation – especially if the person was previously friendly with others

- sadness, depression or uncontrollable crying

- being passive with no spontaneous smiles or laughter

- fear or anxiety, especially about being alone or with particular people

- increased tension or irritability or attention-seeking behaviour

- low self-esteem and lack of self-confidence

- changes in appetite and sleep patterns, for example nightmares or insomnia

- self-abuse or self-harm, for example misuse of alcohol, nicotine or illegal drugs, refusing food or medication.

Isolation is a type of abuse

Case study

In Practice

Bill Eastham, aged 92, is a resident in The Brook residential and nursing home. Bill was a prisoner of war for most of the Second World War and has started to have nightmares about this. Michael, Bill's 16-year-old great-grandson, visits him once or twice a week. Jenna, a social care student on placement, noticed that when Michael arrived to visit his grandfather today he sneaked up behind Bill and whispered something in his ear. Bill then became very distressed and started calling out. Before he left, Jenna asked Michael what he had whispered to his great grandfather. Michael looked a little guilty and said 'Nothing really. I say "the Germans are coming" and he gets a bit excited, that's all.'

1. Is Michael abusing his grandfather? If so, what type of abuse is this? If not, suggest reasons why this behaviour is not abusive.

2. Do you think that Jenna should report the incident and Michael's explanation to anyone else?

3. What do you think should happen next as a response to this situation?

Statistics compiled by Action on Elder Abuse indicate that abuse of elderly people occurs mostly in the family home (64 per cent), followed by residential care (23 per cent), and then in hospital settings (5 per cent).

Indicators of financial abuse

Financial abuse can take many forms but usually involves theft, misuse or manipulation of another person's money, possessions or other financial resources. The signs and symptoms include:

- a sudden, unexplained inability to pay bills

- a reluctance to spend (even when money should not be a problem)

- no food in the house

- unexplained withdrawals from an individual's bank account

- money, chequebooks, bank cards, credit cards or possessions going missing

- being under pressure to change the terms of a will

- other people showing an unusual interest in an individual's money or property (assets).

Indicators of institutional abuse

Institutional abuse occurs when the policies of, or the ways of working in, a care setting add to the risk of abuse rather than safeguarding people against it. For example, an organisation might force everyone to accept the same fixed care routines. A manager might say 'that's just how things are' when a social care worker or individual questions how things are done.

The signs and symptoms include:

- rigid routines (such as mealtimes and bedtimes) or inflexible visiting times

- activities arranged solely for the convenience of staff and the organisation

- cultural or religious needs not being met

- restricting access to food and drink, toilet or baths

- misuse of medication, for example the overuse of sedation to help staff rather than the individual

- lack of privacy, dignity or respect

- restricting access to medical or social care

- examples of poor professional standards and behaviour.

think about

Think about your individuals.

How involved are they in making decisions about their support?

Is your service flexible about meeting individual preferences for mealtimes, bedtimes and food choices?

Indicators of self-neglect

Self-neglect can be accidental or deliberate. An individual who is confused or who has memory problems may neglect themselves unintentionally.

The signs and symptoms include a person:

- neglecting personal hygiene

- not seeking medical or social care

- not taking prescribed medication

- overeating or not eating at all

- self-harming, for example misusing alcohol or illegal drugs or cutting themselves`

- not taking exercise

- living in unhygienic conditions that are a risk to health, for example the presence of vermin.

Indicators of neglect by others

Neglect can be passive or active: it may include a lack of attention, abandonment or confinement by family or society.

The signs and symptoms include:

- denial of access to or withholding of health or social care

- denial of individual rights and choices

- withholding medication

- isolating the individual by denying others access to them

- failure to meet the individual's physical, emotional, social, cultural, intellectual or spiritual needs

- failure to provide adequate food, drink, warmth, shelter and safety

- failure in the 'duty of care'

- exposing the individual to risks and dangers.

Factors contributing to vulnerability

An adult in need of safeguarding may be more vulnerable to abuse or neglect because of a variety of factors.

Factors related to the individual who is vulnerable to abuse	Factors related to the situation or care giver that might cause abuse
• Age (young or old) • Isolation • Physical ability or illness creating dependency • Mental and emotional health issues, e.g. dementia, depression, stress • Communication problems, e.g. speech or hearing impairments or learning disability • Behavioural changes, e.g. following a stroke or head injury • Where violence is seen as normal within the environment or relationships • Past history of accusations • Culture or religion • Financial factors	• Prejudice or hostility towards the vulnerable individual • High stress levels or lack of support for the care giver • Care-giver is drug or alcohol-dependent, or has physical or mental health issues • Care giver has previously been abused themselves • Lack of understanding about the individual's medical or emotional condition • Lack of leadership and clear roles, responsibilities, policies and procedures • Lack of training or poor monitoring of care provision • Staff shortages

Vulnerable people need to be protected from abuse

Factors contributing to vulnerability to abuse

Case study

In Practice

Mrs Porter is an 83-year-old woman who lives alone. Her health and memory have deteriorated since her husband died two years ago. She has no other family. Mrs Porter receives two visits a day to provide personal care and support at mealtimes.

You haven't visited for two weeks and you are covering as the usual carer is off. You are worried when you see Mrs Porter. She has lost weight, her hair and clothes are dirty, and she seems frightened. When you move towards her, she puts her arms up in front of her face. When you ask if she would prefer a wash or a shower, she says the usual carer doesn't bother. When you undress her, you are shocked to find her body is covered in bruises. When you ask about the bruising, Mrs Porter starts crying: 'I don't like him! He hurts me.' She then tells you that 'he' is the male carer. You then find there's little food in the fridge and cupboards, even though shopping is part of Mrs Porter's care package.

1. What signs and symptoms lead you to suspect Mrs Porter is being abused?

2. What types of abuse are taking place?

3. What factors have made Mrs Porter vulnerable to abuse?

Elderly people can be vulnerable to abuse

4.2 Responding to suspected or alleged abuse

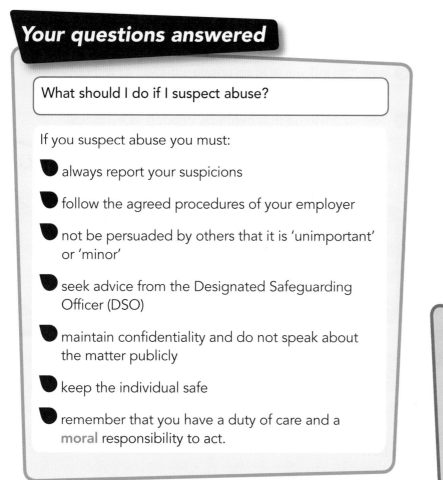

Your questions answered

What should I do if I suspect abuse?

If you suspect abuse you must:

● always report your suspicions

● follow the agreed procedures of your employer

● not be persuaded by others that it is 'unimportant' or 'minor'

● seek advice from the Designated Safeguarding Officer (DSO)

● maintain confidentiality and do not speak about the matter publicly

● keep the individual safe

● remember that you have a duty of care and a **moral** responsibility to act.

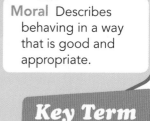

Moral Describes behaving in a way that is good and appropriate.

Key Term

Some incidents of abuse or neglect may seem minor, but when they are linked together they may form a pattern which suggests that abuse is happening. So, if in doubt, always report it.

Reporting a manager or colleague, or a family member or carer of the individual is a very sensitive matter. Always treat this as a professional not a personal issue. If you do nothing, you may allow abuse to continue.

Collude Co-operate with somebody in order to do something illegal or keep it secret.

Key Term

Always report suspected abuse

If you suspect abuse you should **not**:

- ignore it or hide it for fear of the consequences
- **collude** with colleagues or make the situation worse by covering up for others
- jump to conclusions without examining the facts
- confront the person you think is responsible for the abuse
- leave the individual in an unsafe situation or without appropriate support
- destroy anything that might be needed as evidence.

find out!

Do you know where to find the *Safeguarding Adults at Risk* policies and procedures in your work setting? Find out what they say, so you understand what actions to take if you suspect an individual is being abused or if an individual tells you they are being abused.

How to preserve evidence of abuse

You must try to preserve any evidence if you think a criminal offence may have taken place.

Do not:

- move or remove anything from a situation where you suspect or observe abuse
- touch anything, unless you have to make the area or person safe
- clean or tidy up
- allow access to anyone not involved in investigating.

Do:

- record any visible signs of abuse, such as bruising, physical injuries or torn clothing

- avoid touching people or objects wherever possible and do not destroy fingerprints

- preserve clothing, footwear, bedding and similar items, and keep them safe and dry

- record any injuries

- preserve and record the state of the individual and the alleged abuser's clothing, and the condition and attitudes of the people involved

- preserve items in a clean paper bag or unsealed envelope

- preserve liquids in clean glasses.

find out !

Find out more about how to make and securely store confidential records of abuse, such as witness statements, reports, photos and any other evidence.

Case study

In Practice

Paul Heston is a 25-year-old man with learning disabilities. He travels to the day centre by bus from his home where he lives with his parents. Paul arrives late one morning, distressed and dishevelled. His coat is torn and muddy. He has a cut on his cheek and facial bruising. He is limping and holding his side. His rucksack, phone and wallet are missing. He says he was attacked by a group of boys after getting off the bus. They dragged him into the nearby park, where they hit, kicked and punched him. They called him names and swore at him. They then stole his wallet and mobile phone. Paul asked a passer-by for help, but no one came to his aid. He is frightened that his father will be angry with him as his phone is new.

1. What would you do in this situation?

2. Which other agencies are likely to be involved in supporting Paul?

3. How would you preserve any evidence?

4.3 National and local policies and local systems for safeguarding

find out!

Does your workplace have a copy of *No Secrets*? Find out if individuals using your service are given information about *Safeguarding Adults at Risk* procedures. If not, why not?

Two key documents that relate to adults in need of safeguarding are:

- *No Secrets* (2000) – guidance on developing and implementing multi-agency policies and procedures to protect vulnerable adults from abuse

- *Safeguarding Adults* (2009) – a national framework of standards for good practice and outcomes in adult protection work.

The table below summarises national legislation with regard to safeguarding.

Legislation or national policy	Summary of key points
Legal powers to intervene	A range of laws enable abusers to be prosecuted, including: Offences Against the Person Act (1861) – relates to physical abuse Sexual Offences Act (2003) – relates to sexual abuse Protection from Harassment Act (1997) – relates to psychological abuse Section 47 of the National Assistance Act (1948) – relates to neglect.
Human Rights Act (1998)	All individuals have the right to live free from violence and abuse. Rights include: Article 2: The right to life Article 3: Freedom from torture (including humiliating and degrading treatment) Article 8: The right to family life.
Mental Capacity Act (2005)	Outlines five key principles to protect adults at risk who are unable to make their own decisions. Also covers financial abuse.
Safeguarding Vulnerable Groups Act (2006)	Resulted from the Bichard Inquiry in 2002 into the Soham murders and led to the creation of the Independent Safeguarding Authority (ISA) which oversees the vetting and barring scheme.
Health and Social Care (HSC) Act (2008); HSC Act (2010); CQC Regulations (2009)	Established the Care Quality Commission (CQC) to replace National Minimum Standards, and introduced essential standards of quality and safety.

National legislation and safeguarding adults

What roles do different agencies play in adult safeguarding?

The table below identifies a number of different agencies involved in adult safeguarding and outlines their particular roles and responsibilities.

Agency	Key responsibilities
Local authority adult social care services	These agencies: • receive safeguarding alerts • undertake any intervention required to keep individuals safe • liaise/coordinate between all individuals and agencies involved • arrange and record meetings and case conferences • remove the alleged abuser, if required • are represented at police interviews.
All agencies, including: the police, NHS, GPs, medical services, councils, emergency services, independent, voluntary services and charities, private providers, Trading Standards, CQC	These agencies: • work to agreed safeguarding adults policies and procedures • ensure all staff receive regular information about safeguarding training, understand policies and procedures and can recognise signs of abuse • ensure all employees are CRB checked and registered with the ISA prior to employment • inform the ISA of anyone who is unsuitable to work with adults at risk.
The following have additional roles and responsibilities:	
Police	The police: • investigate allegations of abuse if a crime is suspected • gather evidence and pursue criminal proceedings if appropriate • protect people in vulnerable situations.
Medical services, e.g. GP, NHS Acute Trusts	These services: • provide immediate treatment if required • undertake evidential investigations or medical examinations.

Roles and responsibilities of safeguarding agencies

Use the internet to locate one of the Serious Case Reviews mentioned on this page. Read through the key points and findings.

How were the individuals abused?

What types of abuse did they experience?

Who else do you think was abused?

Could similar failures and abuses happen in your work setting?

What reports are available regarding serious failures in safeguarding adults at risk?

As a social care worker, you should understand and learn from the findings and recommendations of inquiries into failures in safeguarding practice. In the past few years there have been a number of these, which have been documented in inquiries and Serious Case Reviews, including:

◗ Margaret Panting Serious Case Review (2004)

◗ Steven Hoskin Serious Case Review (2007)

◗ Michael Gilbert Serious Case Review (2011)

The review findings in each case indicated that:

◗ the fundamental safeguarding needs of each individual were consistently neglected by health, social care and criminal justice agencies

◗ staff employed by various agencies ignored or failed to recognise the individual's rights and need for protection

◗ poor communication, planning, coordination and thoughtlessness left each individual in an abusive and dangerous situation

◗ lack of coordination, information-sharing and integration between agencies resulted in the safeguarding needs of vulnerable individuals being overlooked or neglected.

Tip

It is important to research any organisations before you interview with them. Look at their website and local press to see if they have made any comments regarding to safeguarding or other issues. You can impress your interviewer by bringing these articles up in discussion.

Your role in safeguarding and protecting against abuse

There are various different sources of information and advice on your role in the safeguarding and protection of the individuals you support and care for.

As well as your workplace's policy documents, you should have training, updates and regular supervision sessions on types, signs and symptoms of abuse. These should help to give you confidence in your ability to perform this important part of your social care role.

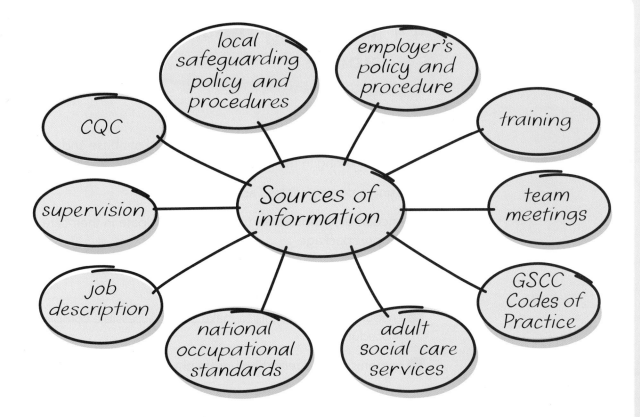

Sources of information and advice about your role in safeguarding vulnerable individuals

Safeguarding – Coventry City Council

Safeguarding is everyone's responsibility, from relatives and carers to directors and inspectors. If you view safeguarding as a jigsaw, you can see that each individual needs to report and record their accurate information in order to form a full picture. It is therefore essential that our employees take safeguarding seriously to provide a full picture which could prove to be key in the safeguarding of our individuals.

4.4 Reducing the likelihood of abuse

Social care workers can reduce the likelihood of abuse and neglect occurring in their workplace by:

- using a person-centred approach to care
- encouraging individuals to actively participate in their care or support package
- allowing individuals in the care setting to make their own choices
- encouraging individuals to make use of accessible complaints procedures
- recognising and reporting unsafe practices.

Person-centred approaches

Person-centred approaches are particularly effective when supporting adults with learning disabilities, adults with mental health problems and individuals with dementia. Every individual has their own unique and different life story, needs, wishes and values. It is important to understand these as a way of putting the person at the centre of the care planning and delivery process. Person-centred approaches are covered in detail in Unit 7.

think about

Think about the individuals who you support. How do you show that you see each of them as a unique individual? What do you do to ensure you understand their point of view, wishes and expectations? How do you keep them involved in decisions about their own support and care?

Encouraging active participation

The main result of 'active participation' is the empowerment of the individual concerned. The individual is given independence, and is empowered to make choices about how their personal support or assistance package is delivered. The individual can then *actively* take part in their own care, instead of just *passively* receiving support in a way that is convenient to the provider. Self-directed budgets, where individuals manage their own care package, are an important part of active participation.

It is important to encourage individuals to actively take part in their care

Promoting choices and rights

You can play an active part in promoting the choices and rights of the people you provide care or support for by spending time getting to know each person as an individual. If you get to know them, you can:

- understand their needs and abilities, like and dislikes

- understand how their condition affects their day-to-day life and activities

- understand what is important to them and what their priorities are

- understand how their past experiences impact on their views and current situation

- respect their uniqueness and personal values.

Encouraging use of accessible complaints procedures

Complaints are a very important form of feedback. Being open to feedback means that a social care organisation can review and improve its procedures for the detection of abuse. Social care organisations must develop complaint procedures that are accessible, easy to understand and user-friendly. Individuals and their families should feel able to make complaints without fear of retribution. Accessible complaints procedures should:

- be written in plain English and available in different formats – in pictures, other languages, audio or Braille

Empowerment
Gaining more control over your life by having opportunities to develop greater self-confidence and self-esteem.

Retribution
Something done to injure, punish or 'get back' at someone.

Plain English
Communication styles that are clear, brief and to the point and avoid technical language, particularly in relation to official communication.

Key Terms

- include an explanation of how to use the complaints procedure

- include a way of checking that individuals understand the procedure

- be displayed in public areas of the service

- be provided by staff trained to respond positively to complaints

- encourage individuals to complain if they are dissatisfied with their support

- use a key worker system to ensure individuals are listened to and given the opportunity to complain informally

- confidentially inform individuals using the service when their complaints have been dealt with and what the outcomes are.

4.5 Recognising and reporting unsafe practices

Any practice that puts an individual or care worker at risk could be considered unsafe. Unsafe practice includes not wearing personal protective equipment, not undertaking risk assessments and ignoring strategies to manage risk. Unsafe practice can also result from insufficient resources (lack of equipment, lack of time or lack of staff) and operational difficulties (lack of training, poor leadership or lack of staff supervision).

Unsafe practice
An approach or standard of care that puts individuals at risk.

Key Term

What action should you take if you identify unsafe practices?

You have a duty of care to tell your employer about any unsafe practices and to take action to protect yourself and others. You should:

- make any hazardous situation safe where it is possible to do so (for example, use a hazard sign to identify an unsafe environment)

- ensure others are aware of the potential danger – if appropriate, remove and label broken equipment

- report the situation verbally and in writing without delay to the person in charge, completing any incident or maintenance forms that are used in the workplace

- follow up to check if the situation has been dealt with effectively.

Safety is everyone's responsibility in social care settings. In some situations unsafe practices may have become accepted over time, but as a social care worker you should not accept this as 'normal'. You could lose your job if you ignore abuse or don't follow the correct procedure.

Remember to check local procedures, seek advice and, if necessary, register a complaint if you have concerns about apparently unsafe practices. Doing nothing will only support the unsafe practice.

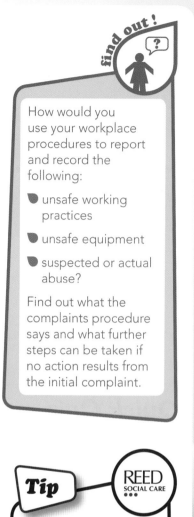

find out!

How would you use your workplace procedures to report and record the following:

- unsafe working practices

- unsafe equipment

- suspected or actual abuse?

Find out what the complaints procedure says and what further steps can be taken if no action results from the initial complaint.

Tip

REED
SOCIAL CARE

Each organisation, and each recruitment agency that you might work for, will have their own safeguarding and whistle blowing policy. You should familiarise yourself with these policies to ensure that you can follow the correct procedure if you ever need to.

Make a hazardous situation safe where possible

What action should you take if there has been no response to reported suspected abuse or unsafe practices?

When you raise a concern and report either suspected abuse or unsafe practices, you should always ensure that you put this in writing. This will allow you to produce detailed, written evidence when your complaint is investigated.

Most complaints procedures include agreed timescales and steps for dealing with a complaint or incident. If you raise concerns about unsafe practices, or report an incident, but the proper timescale for responding to your complaint is not followed, then you should follow your organisation's procedures for grievances. This grievance procedure may involve reporting the situation to a more senior person within the organisation, to the Adult Social Care Services department of your local authority or to the Care Quality Commission (CQC). Depending on the grievance, you may also want to contact your trade union for information and advice.

Quick Quiz

1   Max, a learning disabled man, alleges that one of your female colleagues often strokes and fondles him inappropriately while disguising this as helping him to wash. What should you do?
   a. Reassure Max that your colleague was carefully vetted before being employed.
   b. Phone 999 and report the matter to the police.
   c. Ask Max to describe what happened and report this to your manager.
   d. Make a joke and tell Max to forget it happened.

2   If you suspect that a social care client is being abused in any way, you should:
   a. Keep a file, gathering information together until you have a strong case against the perpetrator.
   b. Inform a senior member of staff, or the person with safeguarding responsibility as soon as possible.
   c. Avoid working with the client in case they accuse you of being involved in the abuse.
   d. Confront the alleged abuser and let them know you are watching and will report them if necessary.

3   A colleague tells you a female client has accused another colleague, who is a good friend of yours, of slapping her for swearing. What should you do?
   a. Speak to the client to find out more about the situation.
   b. Advise your colleague to report the matter immediately to a manager or to the person with safeguarding responsibility.
   c. Avoid the client as she may hit out again.
   d. Gather your colleagues in the staffroom to discuss the matter in depth.

4   Eleni is a community support worker in a dementia care team. When she knocks on the door at the home of her 80-year-old client Ena she is alarmed to hear raised voices, a scream and sobbing. Despite waiting for five minutes and knocking again, nobody answers the door. What should Eleni do?
   a. Phone 999 for emergency services.
   b. Phone her manager for advice.
   c. Report the matter to the Care Quality Commission.
   d. Leave a note saying she will come back later to check everything is OK.

Quick Quiz (continued)

5 A client you care for in her own home has Down's syndrome and tells you to take money from her purse to pay for her shopping. Later, her mother accuses you of stealing money from her daughter. What should you do?

a. Tell the client's mother to call the police if she wants, because you know you have done nothing wrong.

b. Suggest to the client's mother that you call your manager immediately so you can all discuss her concerns about the missing money together.

c. Leave the house at once and write up your account of the incident when you get back to the office.

d. Say that you are angry and insulted by her accusation that you steal from your clients.

6 A social care worker who encourages and supports a client's active participation in their own care and support is:

a. empowering the individual to take control of their own life

b. reducing their own workload

c. giving the individual greater responsibility

d. taking a risk that needs to be carefully managed.

7 Which of the following care strategies reduces the likelihood of abuse or neglect occurring in a social care workplace?

a. Using a person-centred approach.

b. Encouraging active participation of individuals in their care.

c. Recognising and reporting unsafe practices.

d. All of the above.

8 Dee is a youth support worker on a local estate. Several of the young people (aged under 18) who attend her 'healthy choices' group are holding a party at the youth centre this evening. One of them gives Dee some cash and asks her to buy alcohol for them from the local off licence. What should Dee do?

a. Explain that she needs to check first what the guidelines are for having alcohol on the premises.

b. Refuse to buy alcohol and report the matter to her manager.

c. Go to the off licence and buy soft drinks and low-alcohol products.

d. Do as they ask because it will be a really good way to gain their trust.

9 A young woman with learning difficulties that you work with in a community living home has formed a close bond with you, but is now becoming increasingly physical, giving you hugs and asking about your personal life. You think she is sexually attracted to you. What should you do?

a. Let her down gently by explaining that you have a partner, but that you think she's very attractive and will soon find someone else.

b. Tell her very forcefully that you don't fancy her at all and that as a staff member you would never go out with a resident.

c. Return her affection and try to remain good friends with her.

d. Ask for the advice and support of a supervisor or manager about how to handle the situation with sensitivity.

10 A new community care worker visits a client at home only to find the necessary PPE of gloves and aprons have run out. What should she do?

a. Work without gloves and an apron, making sure she washes her hands before and after any personal care procedures.

b. Call her manager to inform her of the situation and seek her advice as to how to proceed.

c. Explain to the client that it is illegal for her to work without PPE and go on to the next individual on her schedule.

d. Use the client's own washing up gloves and cooking apron.

Unit 5

Introduction to duty of care in health, social care or children's and young people's settings

All health and social care workers have a duty of care. It is the very foundation of good, safe practice. Duty of care is very important as it helps to protect individuals in receipt of care and will guide you in your day-to-day work.

This unit explains what duty of care means to health and social care workers and the possible dilemmas that can arise. You will also learn about the link between duty of care and complaints and the importance of responding to and learning from complaints.

On completion of this unit you should:

- understand the implications of duty of care
- understand support available for addressing dilemmas that may arise about the duty of care
- know how to respond to complaints.

5.1 Understanding the implicatons of duty of care

What is duty of care?

As a health and social care worker you have a responsibility to ensure the safety and well-being of the individuals for whom you provide a care service. You are required to work carefully, making sure that anything that you do (or do not do) does not cause harm. This is your duty of care.

Duty of care involves thinking about the consequences of your actions or inaction on other people. It applies to many areas of life; for example, if you are driving a car, you have a duty of care to other road users, including pedestrians, and you must follow the road rules. You are responsible for your actions and must always be able to explain what you have done and show that you have taken reasonable care.

Your duty of care at work

At work your duty of care means that you must work safely and only carry out duties that you are competent to perform. You will be required to undertake regular training and updates. If you are a new employee you will receive introductory training, which is usually called **induction**. Your **job description** will provide details of what your job involves.

Tip

Reputable recruitment agencies, including Reed, will offer additional training courses to people working through their agency. Always enquire about the training a particular recruitment agency may be able to offer you.

REED
SOCIAL CARE

Induction
Introduction to a new work role, including orientation and training.

Job description A written statement that describes the duties and responsibilities of a job.

Key Terms

Key Terms

Standard procedures
Approved ways of working to be followed routinely.

Code of Practice
A set of guidelines and expectations that must be followed.

In your workplace there will be policies and agreed standard procedures that must be followed by all staff. There may also be a Code of Practice which describes the required standard of behaviour and provides guidance on ways of working. If you are uncertain about any aspect of your work, then you must ask straight away.

think about

Consider how to work safely, for example:

- working within the boundaries of your job role, doing only what you are trained and employed to do
- what you are doing and why – be prepared to explain your reasons
- your own limitations
- being assertive and saying what you can and cannot do.

did you know?

At work you have a duty of care to all individuals who use your care service, your colleagues and the public. Your employer and colleagues also have a duty of care to you.

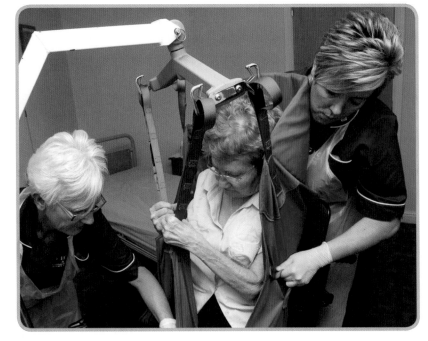

Always ask for the support and guidance you need to do your job safely

Case study

In Practice

Debbie is a new staff member and very keen to help. Another member of staff asks Debbie to assist a frail, elderly female client to wash and explains that a feeding tube is going into her stomach. Debbie is asked if she knows what to do. Debbie isn't sure, but doesn't say anything. She agrees to help. However, as she assists the client, Debbie accidentally pulls the tube out.

- If a care worker does something they are not trained to do, the results can be very serious for both the worker and the individual.

- If the care has fallen below the necessary standard, this is sometimes described as a breach in the duty of care.

- If duty of care is breached due to actions or lack of action (omissions), then an individual can bring a legal case for **negligence**.

Debbie tried to do something that she was not trained to do.

1. Was the client negatively affected by Debbie's actions?

2. How would you feel if you were Debbie?

3. How would you respond if you were asked to do something that you did not know how to do?

Part of your duty of care is to make sure you do the training you need in order to work safely. This will include:

 introductory training (induction)

 mandatory training

 equipment training

ongoing training.

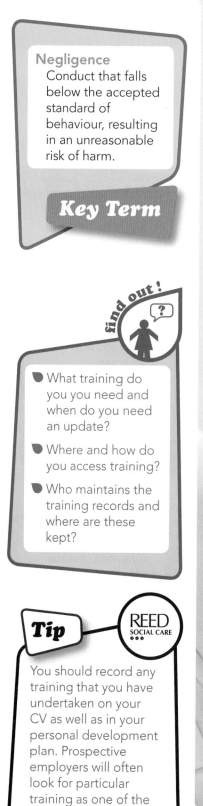

Negligence
Conduct that falls below the accepted standard of behaviour, resulting in an unreasonable risk of harm.

Key Term

find out!

- What training do you you need and when do you need an update?

- Where and how do you access training?

- Who maintains the training records and where are these kept?

Tip

REED
SOCIAL CARE

You should record any training that you have undertaken on your CV as well as in your personal development plan. Prospective employers will often look for particular training as one of the first requirements.

5.2 Dilemmas that may arise and where to find support

Describe dilemmas that may arise

There are many risks in everyday life. Care workers may sometimes feel worried about individuals undertaking certain activities because of the risk of harm and the possibility that the worker may be seen as negligent and get blamed if things go wrong. Duty of care should not be used as a means of restricting the freedom and choices of individuals receiving care. Duty of care involves managing risks and, at the same time, promoting individual freedom and choice wherever possible.

If an individual wishes to make a choice or decision, you must respect it. You may not always agree with their choice but, if it does not break the law, it is their decision and they have the right to make it. The Mental Capacity Act (2005) protects people when they are unable to make decisions and provides guidance to health and social care workers.

Within all care settings there should be policies and protocols which establish safe ways of working. If these are followed, staff are protected and individuals can be empowered. Staff can feel confident that they are fulfilling their duty of care to the individuals as they are correctly balancing health and safety issues with individual rights and choices.

What would you do?

Imagine you are a key worker for two young people.

- The young person with a learning disability wishes to go online to chat and surf the internet.
- The young person with **cystic fibrosis** wants to go on holiday abroad alone.

Cystic fibrosis An inherited disease affecting the lungs and digestive system. The body produces abnormal sticky mucous resulting in chronic respiratory infections and impaired pancreatic function.

Key Term

Tip

REED
SOCIAL CARE
•••

When working through a recruitment agency, your consultant should be available to offer guidance if you have any dilemmas while at work.

Agreed safe ways of working

There are several agreed ways of working that will help you with your duty of care to individuals. These include:

 following workplace guidelines, policies and procedures

- assessing risks

- planning care

- working in partnership

- accessing additional support

- keeping good health and social care records

- undertaking training.

Follow workplace guidance and policies

Raising concerns

Limited time and resources at work may sometimes mean you feel under pressure and unable to deliver the care that is needed. Alternatively, you may observe some bad practice in your workplace. Your duty of care means that you are required to report any concerns to your supervisor and/or tutor. Doing nothing is not an option and is not acceptable.

Raising concerns is sometimes called **whistle-blowing**. This can be a very difficult thing to do, but things will not improve for individuals if the care workers don't speak up when something is not right.

Difficulties and potential conflicts can arise regarding the maintenance of confidentiality and the need to share information. Faced with such a dilemma, you should follow information-handling principles. This means you share information on a strict 'need to know' basis and are always able to justify your actions. The subject of confidentiality is discussed in detail in Unit 1 (see pages 12–14).

Whistle-blowing
Exposing poor practice to try to stop it from happening.

Key Term

Sarah's mother receives home care twice a day. Sarah is concerned about the quality of her care.

> **66** I'd like to believe that when care workers are there, Mum is safe and well cared for, but I'm just not sure.**99**
> **Sarah**

Always fulfill your duty of care by acting in the individual's best interests.

If the workers are fulfilling their duty of care to Sarah's mother, they will act in her best interests by promoting her well-being and safety and giving her choices.

Where to get additional support to respond to dilemmas

Do not think that you have to make difficult decisions alone. Guidance and support are available from many places. The dilemma you are facing may be new to you but your supervisors have experience: they know the policies and procedures and can advise you. There may also be other specialist health and social care workers you can ask for advice on specific issues.

You can find further support outside your workplace. Several organisations are responsible for promoting the safety and well-being of individuals receiving care and also the workers who deliver this service.

Duty of care dilemmas – a national charitable organisation

We understand the difficulties and dilemmas that can arise when providing care, which is why we support our staff throughout their time working with us. Although many new employees find their work daunting at first, by following our policies and procedures properly, and using the support avenues that we offer, it becomes easier to make the decisions that are required on a day-to-day basis. When working here, you should remember that you are never on your own – help is available if needed.

Your questions answered

> **Where can I get help if I am faced with a dilemma in the workplace?**

Within your workplace:

- Refer to your workplace guidelines, policies and procedures.

- Report concerns to your supervisor/line manager and request guidance.

- Work with colleagues and consult the wider health and social care team, for example physiotherapists and specialist nurses.

Outside your workplace:

- Care Quality Commission (CQC) – inspects care services to ensure they are meeting government standards.

- Ofsted – inspects and regulates care services for children and young people and those providing education and skills for learners.

- Professional bodies – set standards and provide guidance and support.

- Trade unions – for example, UNISON, promote the rights of the members of the union.

- Skills sector councils – for example, Skills for Care and Skills for Health ensure that the care workforce is appropriately skilled.

5.3 Responding to complaints

Why you should know about making complaints

Individuals have the right to complain about a care service. They may feel that the care does not meet the required standard; they may even have concerns regarding possible harm or neglect.

Sometimes individuals are reluctant to complain because they fear that this could make things worse. It is important that people know how to make complaints and how to give feedback regarding a care service. They must be assured that all complaints will be dealt with promptly and sensitively. This approach will create openness, as people can raise concerns and staff will have an opportunity to respond and improve practice if necessary. A clear and straightforward complaints procedure will protect the rights of individuals.

Tip

REED SOCIAL CARE

As with safeguarding and whistle blowing, all recruitment agencies and organisations that you may work for will have a complaints policy for you to follow. You should ensure that you make yourself aware of these policies when you start work.

Agreed procedures for handling complaints

All complaints should be taken seriously and accurate records should be maintained. When concerns are raised, a prompt response is vital. Written complaints must be acknowledged within a short timescale, often within two to three days. It is important to find out what went wrong and usually a manager will conduct an investigation. There will be a timescale in which the person who is making the complaint (the complainant) receives a response. The next phase is all about putting things right. When complaints are responded to and resolved to the satisfaction of all involved, it is referred to as local resolution.

Local Government Ombudsman
Independent authority that investigates unresolved or complex complaints.

Key Term

If the complainant is not satisfied with the response, they can take the complaint to the **local government ombudsman**. This is an independent authority that investigates complaints and shares the findings to improve practice.

Your role in handling complaints

Remember that your duty of care is to act in the best interests of the individual and not to harm them by your action (or inaction). If you are faced with a complaint, then perhaps you or your workplace are not fulfilling your duty of care. Whether or not you think the complaint is true or fair, it is important to find out what has happened and why the person feels unhappy with the care that has been provided.

- Listen to what is being said. Don't interrupt and, if they are angry or upset, show that you are interested and concerned.

- Don't get angry or defensive, as this could inflame the situation and make things worse.

- Give the person information and advice on procedures for complaining.

- Explain to the person what you are going to do and then do it.

- Report the complaint to your manager or supervisor and follow your workplace policy.

- Learn and reflect on complaints to improve your practice.

It is important that you know how individuals can make complaints or raise concerns in your workplace.

- What is the complaints procedure in your workplace?

- Do people have the opportunity to provide general feedback or comments and suggestions?

Comments cards or other ways of obtaining general feedback from individuals can be very helpful and can sometimes reduce complaints.

Fulfilling your duty of care:

- Listen to individuals and their friends and family.

- Be observant.

- Reflect on what you are doing and the consequences of your actions.

- Be honest and truthful.

- Keep your knowledge and skills up to date.

- Don't think you know everything.

- Be aware of your working environment as a whole and not just the bit that concerns you.

- Maintain good, accurate health and social care records.

- Speak up if something is not right.

- Learn from complaints.

Swallows Care Home
Please tell us how we are doing

I would like to have music to listen to and.

Comments cards can be very useful for receiving feedback

Quick Quiz

1 Duty of care is important because:
   a. it protects individuals
   b. it makes the workplace safer
   c. it is central to good practice
   d. all of the above.

2 If a worker uses a piece of equipment that they are not trained to use and an individual is harmed, this is:
   a. a breach of duty of care
   b. something that can't be avoided
   c. nothing to do with duty of care
   d. equipment failure.

3 Which law protects people when they are unable to make a decision?
   a. Mental Capacity Act (2005)
   b. Health and Safety At Work Act (1974)
   c. Data Protection Act (1998)
   d. Freedom of Information Act (2000)

4 If an individual in your care wishes to go for a walk but you are worried about them falling, what should you do?
   a. Tell them they can't go.
   b. Physically restrain them from going.
   c. Tell them you will take them later, knowing you won't.
   d. Seek advice from your supervisor and agree a plan of care to support the individual with their wishes.

5 If you observe some bad practice at your workplace, what should you do?
   a. Ignore it.
   b. Join in because it's quicker to do it that way.
   c. Step in to stop it straight away.
   d. Report it to your supervisor and/or tutor.

6 How does training link to duty of care?
   a. Training updates are needed in order to work safely.
   b. Training is relevant to senior staff only.
   c. The more training you have, the less you need to worry about duty of care.
   d. You only need to be trained once.

7 Which of these is the **least** appropriate source of guidance and advice if you require guidance to deal with a dilemma?
   a. Your trade union
   b. Your manager
   c. Your best friend
   d. Professional bodies

8 A person wishes to make a complaint. What should you do?
   a. Listen to what they are saying.
   b. Tell them they need to speak to your boss.
   c. Tell them it's your colleague's fault and that they need to speak to them.
   d. Tell them it has to be in writing.

9 Health and social care services should have a complaints procedure in place because:
   a. it is necessary for freedom of speech
   b. new staff may need to complain
   c. people have the right to complain and need information on how to do this and what to expect
   d. it will look good when inspectors visit.

10 Learning from complaints can result in:
    a. the same mistakes happening again
    b. workers avoiding tasks linked to the area of the complaint
    c. an open and honest working environment
    d. individuals losing trust and confidence in the service providers.

Understand the role
of the social care worker

This unit will introduce you to the knowledge and skills needed to understand working relationships in social care settings. It will also look at the importance of working in ways that are agreed between you and your social care employer and of working in partnership with others in the social care sector.

Effective and appropriate relationships are central to the role of social care workers. As a social care worker you will need to become skilled at forming and maintaining work relationships with a variety of other people, including individuals, their family members, colleagues and other health and social care professionals. Effective social care workers do not confuse working relationships with friendships or other types of relationship that they have.

On completion of this unit you should:

- understand working relationships in social care settings
- understand the importance of working in ways that are agreed with your employer
- understand the importance of working in partnership with others.

6.1 Understanding working relationships in social care settings

Social care workers are employed in a variety of different settings. In every social care setting the ability to form and maintain effective working relationships with clients, their carers, families and partners, as well as with colleagues, managers and other care providers, is central to everyday work activities.

You will need to use your relationship-building skills to provide support and assistance to others and to work co-operatively and effectively with a range of other people. At first glance this might just seem like common sense. However, it requires skill and will improve as you develop your knowledge and experience of social care practice.

There are approximately 1.5 million social care workers in the UK workforce. This number is expected to grow significantly over the next 15 years.

Different types of relationships

Experienced and skilled social care workers understand that they have several different types of relationship with others. These include:

- family relationships with parents, brothers, sisters and other relatives
- friendships
- close, personal, romantic and intimate relationships
- working relationships.

Each type of relationship serves a different purpose and meets different needs, both for you and for the other people involved. The expectations, rules and relationship boundaries that apply to your friendships are not the same as those that apply to your work relationships. The distinction between work-based and other personal relationships is particularly important in social care work.

What different kinds of relationships do you have in your life? Which ones are most important to you? Which ones have most influence on your life?

Understanding personal relationships

The personal relationships of social care workers are likely to include relationships with others who are family members, friends or a partner with whom you have a close personal, romantic or intimate relationship. Each of these relationships can be classed as a non-work relationship, although they are also different from each other.

Family relationships

Family relationships tend to be based on a deep emotional bond that gives a person a lasting sense of belonging and security. In fact, a baby's first relationship with his or her parents or main care giver is called the **attachment relationship**. It is through this relationship that people learn to feel loved and secure. An effective attachment relationship is necessary for a person to develop a sense of emotional security and confidence.

did you know?

People aged between 35 and 54 spend most days or every day with their family. People aged between 16 and 24 spend the least time with family members.

(Office for National Statistics, 2011).

It is through family relationships that people tend to learn about attitudes and values, develop communication and social skills and work out how to provide care and support for others. This is known as **socialisation**. Family relationships also tend to have a strong influence on a person's self-esteem and self-concept (how they feel about themselves).

Tip

You might provide informal care to friends or family throughout your life. Examples of this can be useful to prospective employers – remember to make a note of examples of this kind of care to provide in an interview situation.

Attachment relationship A relationship that is based on strong emotional bonds.

Socialisation The way in which a person learns about the world around them, and the values and expectations of the society they live in.

Key Terms

Early family relationships have a lasting impact on your life

A person's early relationships in childhood are thought to provide a model (or 'blueprint') for the relationships they have later in their life. Why might it be important for social care workers to understand this?

According to data collected by the Office for National Statistics in 2011, 68 per cent of people aged 16–24 spend most days or every day with friends.

Friendships

The bonds of friendship are different from the bonds people form through family relationships. They tend to be based on liking another person who you connect with and who has similar attitudes, values and interests to your own.

Friends may feel they have a strong emotional connection to each other. But it is always possible to choose who you spend your time with and to change your friends if they don't meet your needs or are no longer fun to be with. Family relationships, on the other hand, are more permanent, less voluntary and more deeply rooted. Ultimately a friendship should help to boost your self-esteem and confidence and contribute positively to the way you feel about yourself as a person.

Friendships play an important part in a person's social and emotional development. They provide you with your first relationships outside the family and require you to give as well as receive social and emotional support. Throughout your life, friends help to shape who you are, what you feel and how you relate to others: they affect your personality, social skills and emotional development.

Friendships support you, make you feel that you are liked and wanted and help to provide a feeling of belonging. Friendships are based on emotional bonds but are better thought of as relationships that connect everyone to a social group.

Close personal, romantic and intimate relationships

People usually become interested in close personal, romantic and intimate relationships in their early teens. As teenagers or adolescents, individuals can fall in and out of love quickly. Becoming romantically involved with another person can feel exciting and helps to make you feel good about yourself. Being rejected, or not having your feelings returned, can be painful, but it is a good way to learn more about yourself and what you are looking for in a relationship.

Close personal, romantic and intimate relationships tend to be more emotionally intense and physically intimate than friendships. The emotional and physical boundaries of these relationships are significantly different from those of other friendships and family relationships. These relationships tend to require a greater degree of personal trust and emotional commitment than friendships or work-based relationships.

Case study

In Practice

Bina is a 22-year-old social care worker, employed by a local authority. She currently supports older people living in the community but is a bit bored with her job. She has recently told a colleague that 'it's all old ladies, mashed food and lost handbags'. Bina is keen to apply for a support worker post at a local night shelter for homeless people. She told her colleague, 'At least the users are more my age and some of the *Big Issue* blokes are quite … well … quite nice, aren't they!'

1. What do you think about Bina's motives for applying for the post she is interested in?

2. What might you say to Bina about relationship boundaries as a way of reminding her of the social care worker role?

Tip

REED
SOCIAL CARE
●●●

Prospective employers will always want to know 'why' you wish to join their organisation, and why you want the role you have applied for. You should think about and discuss your motives for applying for a job with your friends and family prior to the interview process.

Just over nine out of ten (91 per cent) UK workers reported that they were satisfied with their working relationships. This is slightly higher than the 87 per cent satisfaction rating of workers in the rest of Europe.

Tip

REED
SOCIAL CARE
•••

You will often have more of these qualities than you may realise. Remember to sell yourself to your employer at interview – these skills are just as important as other practical skills that you may have.

What would you do?

If you were at an interview for a social care worker job, which of the qualities or skills listed in the diagram opposite could you say you currently have or are able to contribute to teamwork situations?

Working relationships

Working relationships are different from the various types of personal relationships. The main difference is that they are not personal: they are all about working together with others to achieve tasks or goals in an organisation. Most working relationships are between people at different levels and have clear boundaries and dividing lines. The boundaries between different workers are set out in each person's job description and in the arrangements for line managements (who reports to who). This means that workers have different levels of power, authority and responsibility in working relationships. For example, as a social care worker you may have working relationships with:

- your employer, supervisor and manager

- your colleagues or co-workers

- other members of a social care team

- workers from different professional backgrounds

- the partner and family of the individual receiving care, assistance or support.

Effective working relationships are usually based on clear communication, trust and respect between the people involved. Some of the qualities of working relationships are shown in the diagram below.

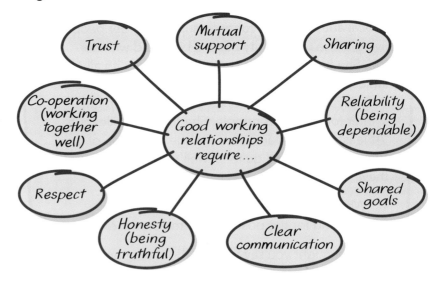

Elements of good working relationships

Employer/employee relationships

You have a formal relationship with your employer. This means that the relationship is based on agreed rules and expectations about how both sides should work together. In particular, an employer has the power to manage the work-related activities of their employees. In turn, employees are expected to understand, accept and carry out the agreed ways of working in their workplace.

Your manager or supervisor is the person who represents the interests of your employer. Your employment contract, as well as the policies and procedures of your workplace, should clearly set out the expectations, rules and boundaries of your relationships with your employer, manager and supervisors.

Formal relationship
A relationship that is based on agreed, formal rules between employers and employees and with colleagues in a workplace.

Key Term

Relationships with co-workers (colleagues)

As a social care worker, you will need to form good relationships with your co-workers (or colleagues), as you are likely to work in a care team or multi-agency partnership. Trust, support and co-operating with your co-workers are important aspects of teamwork situations. In social care settings, teams can change quite quickly, as people leave or join, so it is also important to be adaptable, accepting and supportive of co-workers in order to maintain high standards of care provision for individuals.

Being liked, supported and valued by your colleagues will have a positive effect on you. A lack of respectful, effective or co-operative relationships with co-workers can cause major problems within a social care team and must always be avoided or addressed quickly when it occurs. Effective teamwork tends to be based on:

In a workplace employment relations survey (ONS, 2011), 60 per cent of employees rated their relations with management as 'good' or 'very good'.

- clear communication between team members and knowing how you can communicate best with others

- understanding and being open to the contributions made by other team members

- valuing and being open to the differences of others

- carrying out your work effectively so that you 'play your part' in the overall team effort.

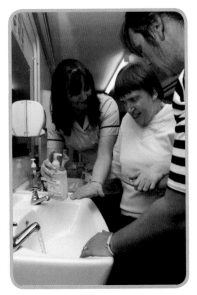

Mutual support helps everyone to do a better job

Relationships between co-workers should be supportive. The best way to make this happen is to look out for others and notice when they are:

- feeling stressed or worried by work or personal problems
- performing their work effectively
- under pressure and having difficulty coping with their workload.

Effective social care teams are made up of co-workers who are supportive of each other. This means sharing information, showing new or less experienced colleagues how to do things and helping out when your co-workers are under pressure or need help. If you help others, they are more likely to help you too – this is mutual support!

find out!

Who are the most supportive people in your workplace? Think about why these people are more supportive than others. Why do you think they act in this supportive way?

Professional relationships with others

Social care workers have contact with a range of other people in the workplace who are not their manager, supervisor or co-workers. These include people who provide specialist care (for example, nurses, psychologists, speech and language therapists or doctors) or support (for example, teachers, legal advocates or housing staff) for individuals. A social care worker may also have contact with the families of the individuals they work with.

You must manage each of these relationships in a professional way, so that others are confident in your ability to work within the agreed guidelines of your role and to focus on the needs, wishes and preferences of the individuals you provide care or support for.

The qualities needed for effective teamwork always apply to these working relationships. You should always focus on the care-giving goals and the agreed boundaries and limitations of your work role when responding to or providing assistance for other care professionals and the relatives of those receiving care and support.

6.2 Working in ways agreed with your employer

The working relationships that you have with others in your social care setting are strongly influenced by your job or work role. This will be defined by your job description, which explains:

- the responsibilities of your job

- who will supervise you and who you report to (line management)

- the nature of the setting where you work

- any other supervisory responsibilities or managerial aspects of your work role.

Adhering to the scope of the job role

Your job description forms part of your contract of employment. When you sign this contract you accept:

- the responsibilities that go with your work role

- that you will work in ways that have been agreed with your employer

- that you will abide by the laws, codes of practice and regulations that apply to social care settings.

Do you know what your job description says about your work role? When was the last time you actually looked at it? Have a look at it now and think about whether your job description actually describes what you do in your workplace.

Tip

Ensure that you ask questions about the job description at interview, so that you understand fully what you will be required to do on a day-to-day basis. Not only will this ensure that you make an informed decision about whether to take a job, but it demonstrates an interest in the position to your prospective employer.

Role boundaries, limitations and accountability

Your job description and contract of employment define the boundaries and limitations of your work role as well as your duties and responsibilities. When you sign your contract you are agreeing to work within the scope of your job role. This is important because your employer (and co-workers) will assume that you will make a professional commitment to do your job to the best of your ability and that you will not go beyond what is expected and what you have been trained to do.

You have a defined work role because your employer needs you to carry out particular work activities in your work setting, contributing, alongside colleagues, to the overall work goals of your social care organisation. Effective care provision depends on each person understanding their professional boundaries and working within their professional limitations.

Once you have completed your induction, your employer will hold you accountable for the effective performance of your work role. That means you will be expected to carry out your job description and to provide care and support the expected standard for individuals. Sometimes your manager may need you to take on extra tasks, but you should always make sure that you are able, qualified and experienced to do the work.

Accountable
Answerable to someone or responsible for some action.

Key Term

How will your employer assess your work performance? Find out about the appraisal system used in your work setting and what you have to do to demonstrate that you are competent and performing to the expected standard.

Agreed ways of working

Your employer will have a range of written policies and procedures about how to provide support, assistance and care in different situations for the individuals who use your care setting or services. These should include clear guidelines on aspects such as the following:

- health and safety

- equal opportunities and inclusion

- confidentiality (keeping things private)

- data protection (keeping information secure)

- supervision

- waste management

- moving and handling

- managing medication

- security and safeguarding.

Each setting has policies and procedures to follow

You should know where to find your organisation's policies and procedures, understand what they say and know how they affect your work role. Policies tend to give general guidance, while procedures give more specific instructions about what to do in defined situations. For example, the moving and handling policy may say 'No manual handling of individuals', whereas the moving and handling procedure should explain in more detail how to use lifting aids or equipment. Following the policies and procedures will ensure that you are working in the safest and most effective way.

find out!

Do you know where to find the policies and procedures in your work setting? When was the last time you looked at them? Can you explain the day-to-day impact of different policies and procedures on your job role?

Case study

In Practice

Eva is a 46-year-old woman with a long history of mental health problems. She lives alone, has no friends and only sees her brother and sister at Christmas when they visit her flat. Jonathan, a community social care worker, is Eva's new key worker. Officially he should make appointments to see her every fortnight or when she contacts him, but he has started to 'pop in' to see Eva most evenings on his way home from work. Eva likes his company but isn't confident enough to say that he shouldn't come so often.

1. Do you think that Jonathan is adhering to the scope of his job role?

2. Which activities described in the case study are likely to be outside his job description?

3. Explain why Jonathan's approach to supporting Eva may be seen as problematic and inappropriate by his supervisor or managers.

REED
SOCIAL CARE
●●●

Working in ways agreed by your employer – a leading housing organisation

Each of our employees plays an important part in our organisation. The reason we work so well together is because everybody knows what is expected of them and follows these expectations. When people don't do what they have committed to do or they try to do too much, this always leads to problems. While we always look for helpful, committed employees, it is better to report something that you feel needs to be done rather than attempt to do something that you are not trained for or not expected to do.

@work

6.3 Working in partnership with others

Multi-agency working is a good way of sharing both resources and expertise

How would you describe your role as a social care worker to someone you have just met? Would you say you 'work with' people or 'do things for' people? In the past, it used to be that you would 'do things for' people in care settings. Now you are expected to work in partnership with the people you support. There are many kinds of partnerships in the social care field, including with:

- co-workers (colleagues)
- practitioners/workers from other agencies
- individuals
- the families and friends of individuals.

Partnerships with individuals

A big part of your role as a social care worker is making sure that people have the support they need to get on with their daily lives. Your relationship with each individual should be based on the idea of partnership – working together in a constructive, helpful and equal way.

Your aim is to support individuals to make their own decisions, if possible, and to do as much as they can for themselves. An effective partnership should allow you to offer and provide more support when it is wanted and needed and less support when it isn't required or desired by the person you are working with.

Teamwork and partnerships

Effective partnership in social care is based on teamwork. Practitioners increasingly work in a range of different groups, known as integrated **multi-agency** and **multi-disciplinary** teams in health and social care settings. This mixed or 'integrated' way of working means that you get people with lots of different skills and specialisms working together to provide high-quality care for

find out!

What different kinds of partnerships are there in your day-to-day work? Think about all the other people you work with and the agencies or organisations who work with your employer's organisation or agency.

Multi-agency working An arrangement where workers from different agencies or organisations work together.

Multi-disciplinary working This is where different care professionals work together in the same team.

Key Terms

individuals. Multi-agency working is a good way of sharing both resources and expertise – and it also saves time and money for service providers.

Tip

REED
SOCIAL CARE
●●●

Remember that if you leave an organisation for a new job, your previous employers will be providing a reference for you. It is important to maintain good professional working relationships throughout your career. Also remember that you may find yourself working with – or for – former colleagues again in the future!

Is your care setting a multi-disciplinary or multi-agency environment? Do you come into contact with practitioners with different training backgrounds and areas of expertise? To find out more about how you all work together, you could ask some of the people you work with about their own job roles and skills.

Partnership working within multi-agency teams, and with co-workers or other professionals in a social care setting, requires a clear understanding of, and agreement on, issues such as:

- communication
- sharing information and confidentiality
- decision making procedures
- each practitioner's role and responsibilities
- how to resolve conflicts
- the goals or objectives of a care or support package.

Open communication between team members is vital for effective partnership working. For example, there should always be open and clear discussions about the needs of individual individuals and the shared goal that everyone is trying to achieve. After all, it makes sense to agree on things if you are working in close partnerships.

It is also important to have clear processes for decision making that everyone understands and complies with. If team members are regularly left out of the decision making process, they may come to feel rejected or demotivated. Even where it is the more senior people in an organisation or agency who make decisions, there should be a chance for everyone employed in a social care setting to put forward their opinion. This helps to build stronger feelings of teamworking.

Case study

In Practice

Phil is 26 years old. He has Down's syndrome, depression and has recently been diagnosed with diabetes. Phil likes to be active and attends a local day centre run by a learning disabilities support group. He sees his GP once a fortnight and has a community support worker who meets him every week. Phil's GP has said he will arrange for a specialist nurse to help him to manage his diabetes.

1. Identify the different forms of care that Phil receives.

2. Which care practitioners could be considered members of Phil's 'care team'?

3. How might Phil benefit from a partnership approach to his care?

find out!

Read a care or support plan that has been written for an individual in your setting. Think about the different care workers involved in providing care, support or assistance for the person: how does this plan reflect the differing roles of different practitioners?

Resolving conflicts

When health and social care workers are working closely together in teamwork situations, there can be conflicts or tensions between different practitioners or agencies. Different approaches and views about priorities do occur in care teams. It is important to have clear procedures about how to resolve these situations so that individuals' interests are not affected. Showing respect to other health and social care workers and learning to understand their work roles, professional responsibilities and priorities helps to create and maintain good working relationships in care teams that use a partnership working approach.

Your questions answered

How should I deal with conflict at work?

If you find yourself involved in a dispute or conflict with another care worker, remember that this is about work – it's not a personal argument. You should always keep hold of your own professional standards, even if others are being unhelpful or difficult. Remember, even if you have a very different opinion from someone else, you should communicate clearly and remain polite. As a social care worker you should always:

- value the different skills, input and opinions of others
- acknowledge (or take on board) the efforts and contributions of other people.

The first rule in any situation where there is a conflict of opinion or approach is, of course, that everyone should stay calm and remain professional. The main skills and approaches needed for resolving workplace conflicts include:

- managing your own stress
- remaining calm when under pressure
- being aware of both your own and other person's verbal and non-verbal communication in a stressful situation
- controlling your own emotions and behaviour
- avoiding threatening others, even when you feel frightened or very angry with them
- paying attention to the feelings being expressed (as well as the words spoken) by the other person
- being aware and respectful of social, cultural and value differences between you and the other person

- developing a readiness to forgive and forget
- being specific and clear in the way you communicate
- having the ability to seek compromise
- trying not to exaggerate or over-generalise
- avoiding accusations
- listening to others in an active way.

Accessing support and advice

You may need support or advice about partnership working when it comes to:

- sharing information
- issues of confidentiality
- explanations of roles and responsibilities
- professional boundaries
- understanding agreed ways of working.

You can obtain advice and support on these subjects from different sources. The first step is to talk to your manager, supervisor or senior colleagues. Don't worry about asking others for help: your manager or senior colleagues will see this as a positive, professional step, not as a sign of weakness. When thinking about asking others for information or help in understanding an issue, remember to consider the needs of the people you care for.

You should also look at your organisation's policy documents. These provide written guidance and should give you lots of information on issues relating to partnership and teamworking. You can find support and advice from other places, including:

- mentoring organisations
- independent advisory organisations
- trade unions
- occupational health services (at your workplace).

What would you do?

How do you think you would respond if you ever became involved in a conflict or disagreement with a colleague in your work setting? How would you try to resolve it? Are there any support or advice services that you could use in this kind of situation?

If you need support, the first step is to talk to your manager

Quick Quiz

1 Which of the following are an example of working relationships?
   a. Sibling relationships
   b. Friendships
   c. Employer/employee relationships
   d. Romantic relationships

2 How are working relationships different from personal relationships?
   a. They involve intimate physical contact.
   b. They are focused on a clear organisational task or goal.
   c. They are always very short-term.
   d. They are more emotionally intense.

3 Which of the following are an example of formal relationships?
   a. Parent and child relationships
   b. Attachment relationships
   c. Relationships with co-workers/colleagues
   d. Marital relationships

4 Working relationships with people employed by other care organisations occur in:
   a. partnerships
   b. multi-agency teams
   c. multi-disciplinary teams
   d. personal care work.

5 The agreed ways of working in a social care setting are outlined in the workplace:
   a. policies
   b. protocols
   c. procedures
   d. all of the above.

6 The scope of a social care worker's role should be outlined in the:
   a. contract of employment
   b. code of conduct
   c. job description
   d. code of practice.

7 Which of the following workplace policies would you consult to find out about agreed ways of working in relation to record keeping?
   a. Health and safety policy
   b. Data protection policy
   c. Security and safeguarding policy
   d. Equal opportunities and inclusion policy

8 Celia, an occupational therapist, Natasha, a social care worker, Davinder, a social worker, and Erin, a housing manager, all work in the same independent living support service. How would you describe their team?
   a. A multi-agency team
   b. A health and social care team
   c. A partnership team
   d. A multi-disciplinary team

9 What is the best response when there is a disagreement about the best approach to take to a care or support situation?
   a. Argue forcefully to get your point across.
   b. Listen, be respectful and seek compromise.
   c. Make a formal written complaint that sets out your position clearly.
   d. Avoid working with the other person to prevent conflict occurring again.

10 Which of the following sources of support and advice about partnership working issues or problems should be available to all social care workers?
   a. A solicitor
   b. An independent advocate
   c. Their supervisor or line manager
   d. A trade union representative

Understand person-centred approaches in adult health and social care

A person-centred care approach is essential to planning and providing excellent care for people who use health and social care services. The themes that run through this book come together when looking at person-centred care: communication; the rights of the individual; duty of care; safeguarding; and using information. You can start by understanding the person's own view of the world, their place in it, their needs and hopes. The skills you have learnt about personal development will support you in using your experiences to improve care. Throughout this unit you can take the opportunity to apply the ideas of person-centred care for a range of individuals in different circumstances and with different health and social care needs.

On completion of this unit you should:

- understand person-centred approaches for care and support
- understand how to implement a person-centred approach in an adult social care setting
- understand the importance of establishing consent when providing care or support
- understand how to encourage active participation
- understand how to support an individual's right to make choices
- understand how to promote an individual's well-being.

7.1 Person-centred approaches in adult health and social care settings

Person-centred values

In Unit 3 you learnt about human rights, equality and diversity. You also learnt that every individual's identity is made up of their own unique set of characteristics. You learnt about the values of giving people choice, privacy, dignity and respect.

These ideas are used to support and encourage the individual to be as independent as possible while working together, in partnership, with health and social care services.

At the heart of person-centred care – designing it, planning it, providing it, evaluating it and making changes in response to that evaluation – are some special principles:

- individuality – the person's special uniqueness
- rights – the person's UK human rights and their rights under UK law and within the policies and procedures of the setting in which their care is provided
- choice – in what care the person has, and how they have it
- privacy – to have conversations and to receive care and treatment away from others
- independence – to live life without interference
- dignity and respect – treating others as you might wish to be treated
- partnership – involving the person as an equal partner in planning and agreeing their care.

Dignity Having respect and status. It is generally accepted that everyone has a right to dignity and ethical treatment. Dignity is closely linked to human rights.

Key Term

Dignity

One of the key principles of person-centred care is ensuring a person's dignity. Every member of the team can make a contribution to this. For example, offering single sex accommodation throughout the NHS has been a priority for many years. There are other aspects of dignity that feature in many areas of health and social care. These include:

- choice and control – providing information and supporting the person's confidence and control in making their own decisions

- communication – really getting to know the person

- eating and nutrition – providing a healthy, balanced diet that the person enjoys, giving regular drinks and giving the person time and support to eat meals ('Protected mealtimes')

- pain management – assessing pain, especially if the person has communication difficulties, and supporting pain relief

- personal hygiene – supporting the person in their hygiene needs and choices; making sure that toilets and bathrooms are clean and private

- practical assistance – working in partnership to find resources that meet the person's needs, such as voluntary sector organisations and support groups

- privacy – this includes separate accommodation for male and female individuals and also the need to provide a separate room for private conversations

- social inclusion – supporting the person in keeping occupied and active and in learning how to use information technology for social contact.

Person-centred approaches

Person-centred planning is a way of working that all individuals should expect. It is of particular importance when working with vulnerable individuals in order for them to feel in control of what is happening. Vulnerable people include those with:

- learning difficulties

- physical disabilities

- mental health issues.

The process of person-centred planning includes:

- person-centred thinking skills – considering the person as a whole, and as part of their own network

- total communication – including meeting the person's communication needs and active listening

- essential lifestyle planning – how their lifestyle contributes to their well-being

- person-centred reviews – evaluating the person's care while paying attention to other changes going on around them.

When you think about the person you support, you need to pay attention to their personal relationships, their home, their interests and working life, their place in the community and their view of the world. By doing this it becomes clear that the person in front of you is part of a network connecting them with the people close to them and their wider relationships.

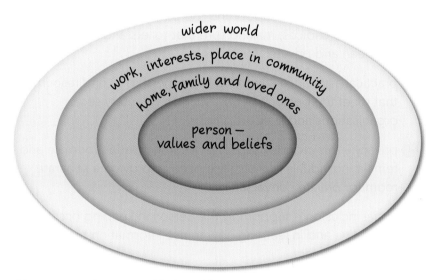

The person at the centre of their world

Essential Lifestyle Planning was developed by Michael Smull and Susan Burke-Harrison in 1996. It is a way of discovering what is important to people in their day-to-day lives. Essential Lifestyle Planning is a way to learn about:

- who and what is important to a person in their everyday life

- how to support the person to have the lifestyle that they want

- how the person can have what is important to them, while staying reasonably healthy and safe

- how to change the service provided to the person, reflecting what is important to the person and how they want to live.

The Essential Lifestyle Plan is developed by spending time with and listening to the person, and by having conversations with the people who are close to them. This information is recorded in the person's plan.

By talking with the person and those close to them the facilitator discovers:

- what a good day is like

- what a bad day is like

- what makes the person happy

- what makes the person sad or upset

- the person's important routines.

Things that are important to the person are then prioritised into three themes:

- non-negotiables or essentials (their 'must haves' and 'must not haves')

- their strong or important preferences

- highly desirable things that the person enjoys but can manage without.

The Essential Lifesyle Plan also includes:

- the person's positive reputation or attributes

- what others need to know to support the person successfully.

Optional sections are:

- negative reputation or issues which need attention

- things that need to be done even if the person does not agree (and pay attention to gaining consent)

- unresolved issues, where there is not enough information or very different views.

The Essential Lifestyle Plan is reviewed as part of the person's ongoing care.

Person-centred review

This takes place at a meeting which considers a range of aspects. Information may be compiled under these headings:

- who is taking part in the meeting

- what people like and admire about the person

- what is important to the person now and in the future

- what has worked well for the person

- what has not worked so well for the person

- the support the person needs to keep safe and healthy

- questions to ask and issues to be resolved

- action planning.

In planning and giving person-centred care, it is important to pay attention to four key principles:

- the person's rights

- independence

- choice

- inclusion.

So, as you learn about the person, the care that you plan and deliver starts to reflect the unique circumstances of the person and the decisions they choose to make.

Carl Rogers and person-centred counselling

Carl Rogers (1902–1987) was an American psychologist. His theory is based on his experience with his clients; he saw people as basically good and healthy, and mental health as part of the normal progression through life. Rogers viewed mental illness and criminality as distortions of that natural tendency.

Rogers' theory is based on the 'actualising tendency', that is, the in-built motivation to develop your potential to the maximum. Rogers believed this to be the case for all living things – not just to survive but to make the best of their existence. For example, weeds will grow through paving, and animals can survive desert and polar conditions.

Rogers used the term 'fully-functioning' to describe reaching a person's best potential. This involves five qualities:

Openness to experience – the perception of your experiences in the world, including your feelings, and the 'genuineness' of self-disclosure, acceptance and empathy (listening and understanding).

Existential living – living in the here and now, or being 'in the moment'. Of course, you can also remember and learn from your past, and plan or dream about the future, while being in the present.

Organismic trusting – trusting yourself to do what feels right and what comes naturally in the context of the acutalising tendency (so not harming yourself or others).

Experiential freedom – the fully-functioning person acknowledges their feeling of freedom, and takes responsibility for their choices.

Creativity – if you feel free and responsible, you will act accordingly, and participate in the actualisation of others and the world as a whole. This could be through creativity in the arts or sciences, through social or environmental concern, parental love or by doing your best at work.

How does your team embed person-centred values into planning and delivering care? Think about:

- the importance of individuality
- appreciation of individual rights
- enabling individuals to make decisions and choices
- the importance of privacy
- empowering individuals to maintain independence and dignity
- treating individuals with respect.

What does the word 'respect' mean to you in terms of the individual's diversity, culture and personal values?

Why is the idea of respect essential to person-centred care?

One of the key aspects of person-centred care that must be considered is **risk taking**. This means enabling individuals to make informed decisions and understand the consequences of their actions, such as:

- the harmful effects of smoking, alcohol and substance misuse
- the benefits of taking prescribed medication
- the advantages of immunisation
- the benefits of a healthy diet and exercise.

REED SOCIAL CARE

Person centre care – a national charity

Person-centred support – placing the individual at the centre of all decisions, and ensuring that the package meets the needs of the individual rather than the service – is a key aspect of social care. This approach to working is promoted throughout our organisation, and we expect all of our employees to understand and support this. While we offer training in this, we also look for employees with the right mindset to support this approach.

@work

Care and support

In health and social care, the individual's assessment and plans for day-to-day care and preferences are recorded with their agreed longer-term goals. This information will be in the individual's care plan. Depending on the type of service, the individual may hold the care plan itself or a copy of the essential information and agreed goals. When writing a care plan, you should ensure it:

- uses an holistic approach to meeting the person's needs and preferences
- uses an individual's own care plans to document their own needs

- pays attention to the detail of the person's individual treatment that is being provided

- shows the importance of applying a person-centred approach when using care plans in terms of the language used and priorities agreed.

7.2 Implementing a person-centred approach in an adult social care setting

Work in a person-centred way

Person-centred outcomes of care are demonstrated by:

- the person being involved with their care

- the person expressing satisfaction with the care provided

- the person's reported feeling of well-being

- care staff working in ways that recognise the person's beliefs and preferences

- achieving a therapeutic relationship that is experienced by the individual and the care staff.

You may find that there are tensions or conflicting priorities that make it difficult to provide the level of support that a person requires within the scope of what services can manage to achieve. However, by fully understanding the individual as a person, it is often possible to find elements of the service that are not required. For example, you might enable a person to buy in ready meals rather than having to pay for someone to cook for them.

Ways of working that contribute to a person-centred approach include:

- working with the individual's beliefs and values

- providing for physical needs

- having sympathetic presence – by engaging with and being truly connected to the person

- sharing decision making when implementing person-centred planning

- always keeping person-centred values in mind.

Tip

REED
SOCIAL CARE

Personalisation is a key issue for all social care organisations at the present time. You should think about examples in your professional and personal life where you have worked or acted in a person-centred way and you should be prepared to discuss this at interview.

think about

Consider what this care worker has to say about the death of Mr Andrews.

'Mr Andrews was brought, on his own, to the A&E department. He had a ruptured aortic aneurysm, and other conditions that meant he would not survive surgery. I pulled the curtains around and put myself in the shoes of his close family so that I could be 'in the moment' with him. Holding his hand, I allowed everything else to drop out of my consciousness while he faded away. There was nothing to say or do; it was a matter of giving that connection or sympathetic presence.'

As you read in Unit 1, excellent communication skills are essential when working with individuals to find out their:

- history (life story)

- preferences in what and how things are done

- wishes that may help to define goals.

Unit 3 describes the importance of working in a non-judgemental way, not discriminating against any individual and ensuring equality and inclusive practice.

7.3 Establishing consent when providing care or support

Establishing consent

When the person is at the centre of their decision making, it is important to be clear about whether the person agrees to the decision or action that is taking place. The action of agreeing is giving consent. It is important to make sure that the consent given is informed consent. This means that the person has made sense of the information needed to make the decision and so the consent is real and valid.

In order to establish consent it is essential to make use of your communication skills:

- verbal – spoken and written

- non-verbal – body language and facial expressions.

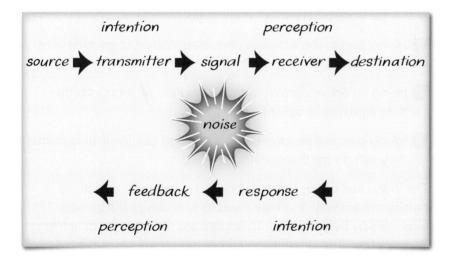

Two-way communication

The communication process includes:

- active listening

- consultation and inclusive communication.

Key Terms

Consent Giving informed agreement to an action or decision. Establishing consent varies according to the individual's assessed capacity to give consent.

Informed consent Permission given in full knowledge of the possible consequences (risks and benefits).

Establishing consent The process of establishing informed agreement to an action or decision with individuals, while ensuring that individuals have access to the appropriate information.

> **❝** A fundamental principle underlying ethical practice is 'informed consent'.**❞**
> **Catherine Dobson**

'Conducting research with people not having the capacity to consent to their participation: A practical guide for researchers', 2008, Leicester: British Psychological Society.

While establishing consent, you need to understand and respect individuals' choices by listening to their questions and concerns and by responding appropriately.

Sometimes it is necessary to resolve conflicts if consent cannot be established. It is important to understand that, in relation to consent, the balance of power should be with the individual but that sometimes it can be difficult for them to make informed decisions. This may mean that you need to seek extra support and advice.

7.4 Encouraging active participation

Active participation

Active participation is about individuals:

- taking part in the activities and relationships of everyday life as independently as possible

- being an active partner in their own care or support rather than a passive recipient

- taking part in their own care by thinking creatively about what they can do for themselves.

The individual needs to be given the power and freedom to participate actively. You may need to encourage the person to do this by helping them to appreciate the benefits of active participation. The benefits could be improvements in the individual's physical well-being or increased independence that improves their emotional well-being and happiness.

Barriers to active participation

Potential barriers to active participation could be:

- learning difficulties
- physical disability
- language barriers.

You need to find ways to reduce barriers to active participation by using:

- physical aids
- communication aids – such as use of language or technological aids
- visual aids.

think about

Consider person-centred care and the special communication needs for a person with autism.

Autism is a developmental problem. It affects the way a person experiences and relates to the world around them and the way they communicate. There are certain traits that everyone with autism shares, while the effects can vary between people. This is why it is described as a 'spectrum'. Some people with autism are able to live independently, while others need help and support throughout their lives.

People with autism have difficulties with communication and social interaction. For example, they often find it difficult to understand jokes, sarcasm and figurative speech, so they may take slang words such as 'wicked' and 'cool' literally. People with autism often have learning disabilities.

Asperger syndrome is a form of autism, usually without a learning disability. People with Asperger syndrome often have a high level of intelligence.

While awareness of autism is growing, and diagnosing children is becoming more common, adults with the condition often struggle.

How would you go about discovering the special needs of an individual with autism when planning their care?

7.5 Supporting an individual in their right to make choices

Making choices

Empowering individuals to make choices for themselves is an essential part of person-centred care planning. The idea of autonomy (independence and free will) of individuals is supported by society's beliefs in human rights. The Universal Declaration of Human Rights was put together by the United Nations after the Second World War. The Declaration includes everyone's rights to dignity, respect, fairness, having their own thoughts and beliefs, security and access to public services.

When supporting a person in making choices, do your best to see things from their point of view rather than from your own.

By being aware of your own attitudes, values and beliefs and the importance of impartiality, you can avoid their personal views influencing a person's decision making and choices.

Tip

REED
SOCIAL CARE
•••

Just as you need to understand an individual's right to make choices, so you must make the right choices regarding your own career. Discuss your options with your family or trusted friends, or with your recruitment agency, in order to make fully informed choices about your future.

Supporting the individual

In order to support people in making choices, you need to spend time and effort in developing respectful relationships. This involves non-judgemental communication and providing information in an inclusive way; ultimately it is about respecting an individual's choices.

Your questions answered

What is inclusive information?

Inclusive information is information that is accessible and available in a range of formats. Examples include innovative learning resources using online solutions and techniques for people with different communication needs (for example, people with dyslexia, sight or hearing difficulties and learning disabilities). If you are working with an individual with specific communication needs, take the opportunity to learn more.

An individual will need time and support to understand their options and the consequences of the choices that they make. Providing this time and support helps to empower the person to question or challenge decisions about them that may previously have been made by other people.

Risk assessment

Risk taking involves understanding and taking responsibility for the consequences of the choices that you make.

In health and social care there are agreed **risk assessment** processes to support individuals in making health and lifestyle choices, or decisions about treatment or care. The process ensures that there is a record that the decision making included giving information and gaining consent.

The individual should be aware of actual or likely danger or harm arising from their choices, for example where the choice increases their vulnerability, or may impact on their treatment or recovery.

The Social Care Institute for Excellence provides guidance for social workers to help individuals make decisions and manage risks.

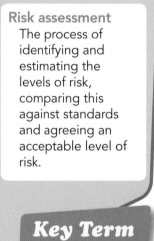

Risk assessment
The process of identifying and estimating the levels of risk, comparing this against standards and agreeing an acceptable level of risk.

Key Term

Key Term

Positive risk taking Taking risks in a deliberate and purposeful way. Sometimes people choose to take risks to improve their quality of life.

Social workers and care support workers are expected to support the individual in identifying and evaluating their own risks. By understanding the individual's history, needs, wants and relationships, the social worker or care support worker can support the person in **taking positive risks**. This includes supporting the person's choices and enabling their risk, while paying attention to the need for safeguarding.

People need support to define their own risks, to recognise and identify abuse and neglect, and clear information about what to do if they are worried.

66 I get to know the person in depth. It enables me to work in a different way – it's more about sitting back and letting them talk more about their lives and what's more important to them, rather than going in and solving their problems for them. 99
Wendy Curry

Social worker at Hull Council
www.communitycare.co.uk

66 People learn by making mistakes. I needed to make mistakes so I could learn. 99
Andy

A young man with autism who made a choice to go to college where he would not be completely protected from risk of abuse from others
www.communitycare.co.uk

think about

How do you go about balancing risk and safety?

It can be challenging to get the balance right between enabling people to take risks while paying attention to the issues of safeguarding and the professional's duty of care.

The idea of risk enablement is key to putting the person at the centre of their care. This has to be underpinned by reliable, consistent and trusting relationships and good communication.

These are some issues you need to take into account when considering a person's risk in health and social care practice:

- factors which increase the person's risk – environment, social, financial, communication and abuse
- the person's ability to recognise the risks
- the person's support and networks to reduce and mitigate the risks
- the nature, length of time and extent of any abuse that has taken place
- the impact of any abuse on the person and other people.

It is worth considering that some people may not tell you something important so that they can take a risk in order to remain independent.

Be aware that, as a practitioner, wanting to avoid risk can lead to you making decisions based on a generalised view of the individual; this does not support person-centred care.

It is important to find practical ways of enabling individuals to define their own risks, and to empower them to recognise and report abuse. This involves excellent communication skills, a trusting and open relationship and time to work through the issues. The individual's own communication preferences should shape the communication process for identifying risks, enabling risks and protecting or safeguarding against risks by supporting informed choice, so that the person is at the centre of their care.

think about...

What is your own attitude to risk taking, for example regarding your finances?

How does this differ from other members of your family?

How do you deal with the differences?

Your questions answered

> Maslow's hierarchy of needs: how do you work out which needs are more important?

Abraham Maslow first proposed his hierarchy of needs in a 1943 paper called 'A Theory of Human Motivation'.

This model explains why a person has to have their basic needs met before addressing their higher emotional needs. The idea is usually illustrated by a pyramid. The hierarchy shows that, in order for people to reach their maximum potential, which Maslow defines as 'self-actualisation', basic physical and psychological needs must be met first. These build upon each other from the base of the pyramid, starting with physiological needs (needs that are vital to survival). At the top of the pyramid is Maslow's idea of 'self-actualisation' (self-awareness and concern with personal growth and fulfilling potential).

Maslow's hierarchy:

- Self-actualisation – personal and spiritual fulfilment; acceptance; creativity (top of the pyramid)

- Self-esteem – status; voicing expertise and experience

- Social – belonging; connection; conversation; affection

- Safety – shelter; protection; security

- Sustenance – basic physiological needs: air, water, food, warmth and sleep (base of the pyramid).

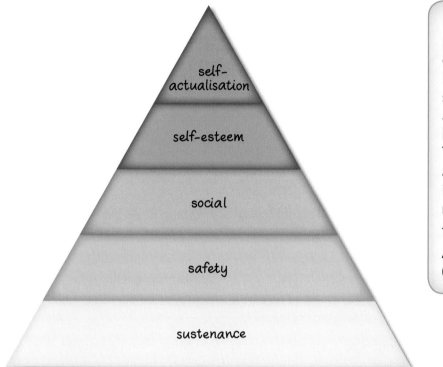

Maslow's hierarchy of needs

> **66** Self-actualizing people have a deep feeling of identification, sympathy, and affection for human beings in general. They feel kinship and connection, as if all people were members of a single family.**99**
> **Abraham Maslow (1908–1970)**

7.6 **Promoting an individual's well-being**

Maslow's hierarchy describes the different levels of needs. Person-centred care involves working with the person to find ways to meet their needs to as high a level as possible in order to achieve the best possible **well-being**. Meeting a person's physical and emotional needs will contribute to a person's health and well-being.

> **Well-being** Factors such as biological, health, spiritual, emotional, cultural, religious and social satisfaction come together to create a person's well-being.
>
> **Key Term**

Promoting well-being

Everyone has a different understanding of what makes up their well-being. This depends on identity and beliefs; and it is easy to see how self-esteem features highly in a feeling of well-being. People have a good chance of feeling good about themselves if they:

- are respected
- are given privacy and dignity
- are encouraged to to be independent
- take part in the traditions associated with their cultural and religious beliefs.

Your own emotional literacy, or emotional intelligence, helps you to be aware of and appreciate another person's feelings and level of well-being.

In order to improve a feeling of emotional well-being for individuals, you should pay attention to the following:

- working in partnership to set realistic and achievable goals
- empowering individuals to develop confidence, feel good about themselves and raise their self-esteem by communicating with positive encouragement and active listening
- helping the person to develop as much independence and assertiveness as they can
- creating and maintaining a positive environment with, for example, interesting activities and pleasant surroundings.

Self-esteem Your belief about your self-worth.

Emotional intelligence Includes self-awareness, impulse control, motivation and empathy – some of the qualities that underpin the outstanding communication skills in those people who have successful relationships at home and work.

Key Terms

Your questions answered

What are personal budgets and how do they work?

Personal budgets are a good example of a person-centred approach in social care practice. Wherever possible, individuals are allocated their own personal budget. This allows the person to choose a combination of services that will best support them in living as independently as possible. Individuals can receive direct cash payments which give them choice and control over the services they receive.

The person may choose to receive a direct payment which they use to pay for services, or they may prefer to choose the care they receive but leave the responsibility for commissioning services to the local authority. They can also choose a combination of the two.

All social care individuals should have a personal budget in place by 2013.

While keeping the person at the centre of these processes, social workers and care support workers have a role to play in the following:

- **decision making** – helping individuals decide whether a direct payment or a personal budget suits them best

- **assessing and allocating resources** – assessing individuals' needs, or supporting them to do this themselves, and allocating a budget to meet these needs, using the resource allocation system that is in place

- **reviewing the size of a personal budget** – if the personal budget appears not to be enough to meet the person's needs, the social worker would take the case to a council funding panel

- **support planning and brokerage** – drawing up a plan with the individual and their family, and providing information on sourcing services to implement the support plan (this is known as brokerage)

- **review** – reviewing the individual's needs for support.

Choices available to the person might include the following (you could think of some more):

- domestic cleaning service

- a dog-walking service, enabling the person to enjoy the companionship of their pet

- a taxi to go to a social club

- gym membership to support a return to fitness

- broadband connection to allow the person to shop on the internet and have their groceries delivered

- an aromatherapy massage.

find out !
?

Spiritual and religious beliefs and traditions can affect how people express some emotions such as love and affection. They can influence what people choose to read, watch on television and the music or radio programmes they listen to. Spiritual beliefs and practices can benefit people's physical and mental health.

Spiritual and religious beliefs may become more important to people when they are ill or stressed. So gaining experience and confidence in talking and listening about the person's faith can be useful in the context of planning and giving person-centred care.

You might want to ask for support from colleagues, their family or religious leaders in order to meet the person's needs.

Remember that people are often happy to talk about their religious beliefs, and won't be offended if you show you are interested.

Why not find someone in your class or team from a different tradition and share some thoughts?

Life Story Network Life Story Network is particularly useful for people with memory difficulties such as dementia, and for people who are depressed or withdrawn.

Key Term

find out !
?

Find out more about life story work at www.lifestorynetwork.org.uk

Your questions answered

What is life story Network?

Life story Network aims to improve the quality of life and well-being of people by enabling them to share the story of their life, in whatever ways suit them. This could be a combination of writing things down, photographs, letters, computer files, memory boxes and audio and video recordings. It places the person right at the centre of their own story, and is a way of creating purposeful and respectful communication between the person and the staff who care for and support them. This in turn enables care workers to fully understand the person, and makes it easier for care to be person-centred.

Memories make up a life story

think about...

The National Dementia strategy recognises the key role that the families of people with dementia play in their care and well-being. Family members provide most of the person's care at home, enabling many to live in their own home for longer. The family member's knowledge and experience of the person also contributes to making them an expert in the person's care. So the value of putting the person and their loved ones at the centre of assessment, care planning and care delivery is clear.

Consider the benefits of the following:

- Providing the first detailed assessment at the person's home with the carer (family member) taking part

- Obtaining the main carer's observations about the progression of memory loss and other issues; ideally by asking open questions

- Providing specific support for the carer, perhaps signposting additional services such as counselling or practical help, and contact details for the local Alzheimer's Society

- Using information prescriptions to assist family members to obtain information about the condition and the local resources available (for more on information prescriptions, visit www.nhs.uk/Planners/Yourhealth/Pages/Information.aspx)

- Following diagnosis, giving the person the opportunity to discuss dementia and its implications

- Providing specific advice about dementia at a local carers' forum – at the same time and place as the memory clinic is held.

Living well with dementia: a National Dementia Strategy, 2009, Department of Health

Your questions answered

What is a stroke, and what special skills do I need when providing person-centred care for someone who has had a stroke?

A stroke is a 'cerebrovascular accident'. The blood supply to part of the brain is cut off, maybe because of a blockage in a blood vessel or a bleed. As a result, the affected part of the brain cannot function.

Around 150,000 people have a stroke in the UK every year.

Strokes affect people in different ways depending on the area of the brain that has been damaged. Symptoms may be numbness, weakness or being paralysed on one side of the body. The person may slur their speech, finding it difficult to find words or understand speech. Some people may lose their sight or have blurred vision, while others become unsteady or confused. Strokes can affect body functions, thought processes and the ability to learn, feel and communicate.

About a third of people who have a stroke make a significant recovery within a month. Most stroke survivors will have long-term problems, taking a year to reach the best level of recovery, and in severe cases have long-term disability. Recovery takes a long period of rehabilitation, as the person learns to deal with the effects of the stroke.

Caring for a person who has had a stroke takes a high degree of person-centredness in care planning and delivery.Rehabilitation is about achieving as independent a life as possible by taking a positive approach to ensuring that life goes on. This may involve helping the person to acquire new skills or relearn old ones, or helping them adapt to new limitations; this is known as re-ablement. Part of the person's rehabilitation includes helping the person find practical, social, and emotional support.

Getting rehabilitation right for people who have had a stroke, especially if this has left them with communication difficulties, is one of the most rewarding services you can offer as a health and social care worker.

Key Term

Re-ablement
Describes the idea of 'making possible again' rather than restoring previous function. It is a little different from rehabilitation because it involves understanding the whole person rather than just what is physically 'wrong'.

Your questions answered

What are assistive technologies, and how do they support people with long-term conditions in a person-centred way?

Most people with long-term or chronic conditions prefer to manage their own condition as much as possible and appreciate any opportunities to do this. Technology is starting to play an important role in enabling people to:

- understand changes in their health condition
- strengthen their sense of responsibility for their health

Technology can also enable individuals to get professional input when needed. There is already evidence that this leads to reduced admissions to hospital and better quality of life. Telemedicine and telehealth – using a combination of technology for monitoring and communication with the health professional – are particularly useful when the person has more than one long-term condition, for example diabetes and chronic obstructive pulmonary disease (COPD).

Technology supporting communication

Assistive technologies Technological solutions that support telehealth, telecare and telemedicine. Examples are blood pressure and blood glucose monitoring machines sending the results by telephone to a healthcare professional, and using email and or Skype to communicate with individuals, perhaps on a more regular basis than would otherwise be possible.

Key Term

Case study

In Practice

Richard lives alone in a small Victorian terraced house with two dogs. He has no close family. He receives a small occupational pension, having retired three years ago for health reasons. Richard has had diabetes since childhood and over the last decade has started to suffer from diabetes related foot problems which led to a below the knee amputation of his right leg. He finds wearing his prosthetic leg uncomfortable so his mobility is limited, and he manages the stairs in his house with difficulty. Richard likes to be as independent as possible and he chooses not to socialise.

The district nursing team supports Richard in managing his diabetes and treats the small ulcer on his left foot.

The social care team also visits Richard twice a week to assist him with his personal care.

This week Richard has refused care from the district nursing and social care teams.

1. What impact could this be having on his overall health and well-being?

2. As a care worker, what actions would you take to persuade Richard to accept the care being offered while maintaining his rights to risk taking and choice?

Your questions answered

How does looking after your equipment support person-centred care?

Everyone knows the importance of having reliable, clean and appropriate equipment available for health and social care individuals. Processes for maintaining, cleaning and storing equipment and for recording loans and returns save time and money, giving individuals the best opportunity to benefit from loaned equipment as soon as possible after it is needed.

This in turn can help to reduce delayed transfers of care from hospital, it supports short weekend visits home as part of rehabilitation and enables some individuals to be cared for at home. This improves their independence, where otherwise they might need to be in a residential or nursing home. So, indirectly, managing equipment properly supports person-centred care.

Supporting transfer out of hospital after a stroke

The NHS Institute for Innovation and Improvement published a report, 'Focus on Acute Stroke', in 2006 which identified a range of success factors in achieving timely transfer out of hospital after a stroke. Going out of hospital as soon as the person is ready helps them achieve as much independence as possible. Planning for this in a person-centred way, by involving them in goal setting, contributes to a positive experience for the person and their family.

If you work in a hospital or a community hospital, you may be involved in planning for a person to go home after a stroke. If going home is not possible the person may need to move into a residential, care or nursing home depending on their needs. As a health and care support worker in either a hospital or the community, you will need to be clear about your role to play in some of the success factors that the report identified.

find out!

Find out about the end of life services offered in your area and how a person's choices are recorded and supported.

In Practice

Some practical contributions mentioned in the report to support person-centred care include:

- Regular multi-disciplinary team planning for discharge
- Reviewing of length of stay and decision not to discharge
- Keeping information on 'white boards' etc. up to date
- Understanding agreed criteria or goals for improvement or discharge
- Understanding access to social services funding
- Supporting prompt assessments for Continuing Healthcare CHC and Funded Nursing Care
- Requesting therapy-led equipment so that is accessible when it is needed
- Medicines to take out (TTO) are ready at the time they are needed
- Supporting the process for supplying a wheelchair from the wheelchair service
- Working with the specialist community rehabilitation team.

End of life care

End of life care helps people who have advanced, incurable illnesses to live as well as possible until they die. This is an area where person-centred care planning really matters. The physical and emotional needs of the person and the needs of their family are identified and should then be met by skilled staff, throughout the last phase of the person's life and into bereavement.

End of life care is usually defined as care during the last year of life, or at the time of diagnosis of a condition with a poor prognosis (likely outcome). Conditions include motor neurone disease, advanced liver disease, cancer that has spread and become incurable and dementia.

Improving the experience of end of life care for patients and their carers is a national priority. It is suggested that most people would choose to die in their own homes if possible, but their wishes are not always known to their loved ones or to those who provide their care. The Dying Matters campaign encourages people to talk to their loved ones about their wishes. Person-centred care includes ensuring that a person's choices about end of life care are known, recorded and respected.

> **66** As the original provider of patient-centred, palliative care, hospice providers have found that high-quality care – delivered in all settings – begins with a conversation with the patient and their loved ones.
>
> The essential character (is) knowing and then honoring the goals and desires of the patient as we provide interdisciplinary care that treats the whole person and not just the illness. **99**
>
> **Don Schumacher**
>
> President and CEO of the US National Hospice and Palliative Care Organization

For further research

Centre for Policy on Ageing:
www.cpa.org.uk

Sector Skills Council for Care and Development:
www.skillsforcareanddevelopment.org.uk

The NHS Institute of Innovation and Improvement:
www.institute.nhs.uk

Independent Safeguarding Authority:
www.isa.homeoffice.gov.uk

The Stroke Association:
www.stroke.org.uk

Mind:
www.mind.org.uk

Department of Health:
www.dh.gov.uk (Putting People First agenda DH 2007)

Quick Quiz

1   Which of the following lifestyle choices is least likely to benefit the person's overall health?
   a. Smoking, alcohol and substance use
   b. Taking prescribed medication
   c. Immunisation
   d. Diet and exercise

2   According to Maslow's hierarchy of needs, which of the following is **not** one of the basic physiological needs?
   a. Air
   b. Food
   c. Sense of belonging
   d. Sleep

3   Why is it important to work in a way that embeds person-centred values?
   a. To complete the assessment as quickly as possible
   b. To support the person's human rights, and equality and diversity
   c. To prevent the person from taking risks
   d. To learn from errors

4   Mrs Abdul lives alone and has mobility difficulties. When planning for her transfer out of hospital, which of these is a priority in providing person-centred care that supports her rehabilitation and independence?
   a. Agreeing with Mrs Abdul for a family member to call in every day to check she is managing and to support her
   b. Installing a stair lift
   c. Getting her a puppy to keep her company
   d. Delaying her discharge from hospital until her mobility has returned to normal

5   Person-centred care depends on which of the following?
   a. Solving a person's problems for them
   b. Letting a person talk about their life and what's important to them
   c. Providing for their physical hygiene needs
   d. Preventing the person from taking a risk

6   Person-centred care involves supporting a person in fully understanding the consequences of their choices. Which of the following is the odd one out and is **not** part of a health and social care worker's role?
   a. The advantages of taking medication that has been prescribed for them
   b. The benefits of a eating a healthy diet and taking exercise
   c. The harmful effects of smoking
   d. Choosing a health insurance policy

7   According to Maslow's hierarchy of needs, which of the following pairs of needs are expressed in the correct order of priority (basic needs being the priority)?
   a. Personal security; water to drink
   b. Shelter; personal growth
   c. Self-actualisation; sleep
   d. Emotional well-being; nutritious food

8   Which of the following behaviours is **not** part of a person-centred approach?
   a. Providing dignity and respect
   b. Offering choice
   c. Giving privacy
   d. Discrimination

9   Which of the following might require particular attention to providing person-centred care?
   a. A person with learning difficulties
   b. A person who is unemployed
   c. A person with a large family
   d. A person who has just come out of hospital

10 Which of the following is most likely to support a person's emotional well-being?
   a. Setting very challenging goals for the person
   b. Developing independence and assertiveness
   c. Admitting the person to hospital
   d. Enrolling the person in an exercise class

Unit 8

Understand
health and safety
in
social care settings

This unit will help you to understand your responsibilities under health and safety law. You will learn how to conduct risk assessments, protect the individuals you care for, keep yourself safe and respond to emergencies.

On completion of this unit you should:

- understand the legislation and different responsibilities relating to health and safety in social care settings

- understand the use of risk assessments in relation to health and safety

- understand procedures for responding to accidents and sudden illness

- know how to reduce the spread of infection

- know how to move and handle equipment and other objects safely

- understand the principles of assisting and moving an individual

- know how to handle hazardous substances

- know environmental safety procedures in the social care setting

- know how to manage stress

- understand procedures regarding handling medication

- understand how to handle and store food safely.

8.1 Legislation and responsibilities relating to health and safety in social care settings

The Health and Safety at Work Act (1974)

This Act provided a basis for all health and safety aspects within a workplace. The aim is to ensure that employees and the environment in which they work are safe at all times and to reduce potential hazards to health.

find out!

Can you research what safety aspects need to be provided under The Health and Safety at Work Act (1974)?

The Management of Health and Safety at Work Regulations (1999)

These regulations introduced the concept of assessing risks before carrying out any activities that might present potential risks to health or safety.

think about

Can you list some activities that may present risks within a health and social care setting? Think about your daily routine and the caring jobs that you need to do for individuals. When you carry out your tasks, how do you ensure that people in your care are kept safe, healthy and secure?

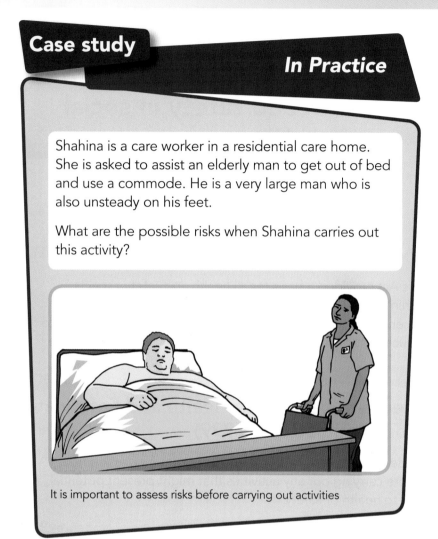

Case study

In Practice

Shahina is a care worker in a residential care home. She is asked to assist an elderly man to get out of bed and use a commode. He is a very large man who is also unsteady on his feet.

What are the possible risks when Shahina carries out this activity?

It is important to assess risks before carrying out activities

Tip

REED SOCIAL CARE

Recruitment agencies may offer training on the Manual Handling Operations Regulations if you work for them. You should enquire about the training which agencies can offer when considering which recruitment agencies to sign up with.

The Manual Handling Operations Regulations (1992)

Shahina will need to assess risks such as:

- the actual task
- the weight of the man and what he is able to do
- how difficult it will be to move him
- the impact of the environment and any space restrictions.

As part of the Manual Handling Operations Regulations (1992), it is a legal requirement for employers and employees to follow these steps of risk assessment to reduce the risk of injury to themselves and the individuals they care for.

Health and Safety (First Aid) Regulations (1981)

This Act requires workplaces to ensure that some staff are suitably qualified to give first aid and that their qualifications are renewed every three years. The Health and Safety Commission and Executive (HSC/E) currently monitor this.

Reporting of Injuries, Diseases and Dangerous Occurrences (RIDDOR) (1995)

It is a legal requirement to report any serious injuries, diseases (such as meningitis), deaths and long-term illnesses to the HSC/E or to the local authority Environmental Health department. Serious accidents that have led to seven days absence from work have to be reported.

Childcare workers must also report serious injuries and illnesses to Ofsted.

Ofsted 'Office for Standards in Education Children's services and skills'. Ofsted's role is to inspect and regulate all services for children and young people.

Key Term

Control of Substances Hazardous to Health (COSHH) Regulations (2002)

The COSHH Regulations (2002) enforce safety rules for storing any hazardous substances such as cleaning fluids, dangerous chemicals and medicines. They also cover the safe use of these substances, the management of spillages and administering medicine, as well as the safe disposal of any hazardous substances or materials.

The main points of health and safety policies and procedures

When you start working in a health and safety setting, you sign a contract to agree to set ways of working. You follow certain standards to ensure the safety and security of individuals, staff members and visitors. These standards are covered in Unit 2 on pages 18–19, but you can revisit them at www.cqc.org.uk or www.dh.gov.uk.

Case study

In Practice

Imagine you are supporting the new care worker Shahina. Copy the table below and describe two or three actions that she must do in the given scenarios.

Scenario	What needs to be done	Who does Shahina tell? What details need to be recorded and where?
84-year-old Molly has a fall		
Henry, who is allergic to fish, has been given fish for lunch		
Mr Allen has soiled his bed		
The hoist appears to be broken		
A man Shahina doesn't recognise is asking for the room of a resident		
Abida says she has the wrong tablets		

Responsibilities for health and safety

Different care workers have different responsibilities. Some of these responsibilities are outlined below.

The social care worker

During any shift you work in health and social care, you must look out for potential hazards and be prepared to take the appropriate actions to report them.

Remember that it is your legal duty to look after yourself and those in your care.

Another legal responsibility is to comply with agreed ways of working: use equipment correctly, do not try to do anything you are not trained to do and follow procedures as set out by the organisation in accordance with the code of practice.

The employer or manager

Employers and managers must provide a written policy for health and safety if they employ five or more employees. Policy documents must set out the responsibilities, arrangements and instructions for all health and safety procedures.

Managers must ensure that new staff are inducted and trained before they carry out any task. They must also ensure that necessary protection (such as gloves) and health checks are available.

Residents or visitors

Residents or visitors also have responsibilities to keep themselves safe and secure and to help the environment to be a safe, secure and clean place.

Special training

> ### What would you do?
>
> If you were the health and safety representative in a home where there are a lot of visitors, how would you promote health and safety?

think about

> Can you describe a practice that helps to ensure safety and security when visitors arrive in the setting?

Case study

In Practice

Shahina is not yet competent to give out medications to residents but Abida has asked her for more pain killers.

Shahina knows the pain killers that Abida is taking, but what are the possible hazards if she gives her some without checking with her supervisor?

What special training may Shahina need?

Other special training includes:

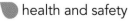 health and safety

 administering first aid

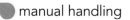 fire safety

 infection control procedures

 manual handling

 food safety.

In Practice

Special training

Copy and complete the table below. Give an example of what might happen if Shahina was not given any training for each of the following aspects of care:

Care aspect	Consequence of performing task with no training
Knowing how to manage an unconscious resident	
Knowing how to give personal care to someone who needs to use the hoist	
Knowing how to operate a wheelchair	
Knowing how to deal with a contaminated dressing	

REED
SOCIAL CARE
●●●

Health and safety – a national housing group

An understanding of health and safety legislation and requirements is a key attribute for each of our employees. This understanding contributes to the safety and security of both our individuals and our employees, so ignoring the rules which are set out could have serious consequences. We would expect any new employee to take the time to understand our rules on health and safety, and to ask questions if they are unsure about anything.

@work

Accessing additional support and information about health and safety

When you begin working in the sector it is very important to ask for help and guidance when you need it. This is especially true when you are asked to do something that you are unsure about. You can refer to written policies and guidance, but you should also seek advice from your mentor or your manager.

8.2 Using risk assessments in relation to health and safety

What do 'hazard' and 'risk' mean?

A hazard is anything that has the potential to cause harm. A risk is the likelihood of a hazard occurring.

Example of a hazard. A spillage that is not cleaned up is a hazard for residents, particularly for blind or partially sighted residents.

Example of a risk. A mouse or insects entering a resident's room though an open window creates a risk to the resident.

Hazard A hazard is an actual threat to one's health or something that could cause an accident such as a spillage of grease where someone will be walking.

Risk The possibility of something potentially hazardous such as an open window near a wasp's nest where a wasp may enter through the window and sting someone.

Key Terms

How many hazards can you find in this community room for residents who have poor vision and are unstable on their feet?

How to use a health and safety risk assessment

There are five steps to assessing risk:

1. Identify the hazard.

2. Establish who could be harmed.

3. Assess the severity of the risk and what control measures are needed.

4. Record the findings.

5. Review the situation as changes occur.

The **control measures** will include any training needed to use the right equipment or to follow correct procedures.

Control measures
Steps to take to reduce possible hazards from occurring.

Key Term

Reporting potential health and safety risks

If you identify a potential hazard, you must report it to your supervisor. Your concerns should also be documented. Ways of doing this include:

- reports to the caretaker (hazards in the environment)
- reports in the care plan (hazards to individuals in your care)
- reports in the accident book – these may be actual accidents or 'near misses' ('incidents').

You must usually include a description of the hazard or incident, and where and when you noticed it. Try to be as accurate as you can and remember to note any action that is taken.

How risk assessment can help address conflicts between an individual's rights and health and safety concerns

There will be times when an individual's rights and choices will conflict with the views of healthcare professionals. You have a duty of care to highlight potential hazards to individuals but, if they decide to take risks with their health, then at least they have the information to make the right choice.

This information and the individual's decision must be recorded. You must also record how the decision and any plans will be implemented and monitored. This is quite a responsibility and you will need to consult with your manager before any final decisions are made, particularly if the decision concerns the individual taking their own medication.

In Practice

There are some general practices, such as wearing disposable gloves and aprons, that contribute to infection control measures. Risk assessments that lead to good practices can show individuals that their right to be protected is being complied with.

8.3 Responding to accidents and sudden illness

Always be alert for a sudden illness. Sudden illness usually requires the quick action from the carer following organisational procedures. A person's life may be at risk.

Procedures following an accident or sudden illness

It is a good idea to attend a first aid course, as this will help you to recognise the signs and symptoms of a deteriorating condition as well as understanding more about sudden illness. Your manager or supervisor will probably arrange this for you, but there are some general procedures that you should know about and follow:

1. Remove any sources of danger and quickly assess the individual to see if they are breathing. You must do this by gently shaking the person's shoulders and asking loudly if they are all right.

2. If there is no or little response, shout for help.

3. Check the breathing by tilting the person's airway back for no more than ten seconds.

4. If the person is not breathing, get someone to call 999.

5. Administer CPR (cardio-pulmonary resuscitation) if you are trained to do this. Currently this involves:

    - opening the airway by tilting the head back

    - checking for breathing

    - shouting for help (to call 999)

    - applying 30 compressions to the chest, followed by two breaths and then alternating this. You need to keep this going until help arrives

did you know?

95% of major slips and trip accidents (in social care settings) result in broken bones. Most slips occur on wet or contaminated floors (see www.hse.gov.uk/healthservices). The research suggests that poor housekeeping, including not cleaning up spillages straight away, can lead to hazards which cause accidents.

find out!

What signs and symptoms may indicate a sudden illness or acute medical reaction?
What are your organisational procedures in the event of a sudden illness?

You must attend first aid courses regularly as procedures for CPR are may change and babies and children require different procedures from those for adults.

If the person is breathing and has some colour in their face (indicating a circulation), then you must put the person on their side (into the recovery position) as you have been trained to do, and stay with the person until help arrives.

You must verbally report your findings to the paramedics or to the GP and then write an accident report. If there are any changes to an individual's condition or a choice or preference has been expressed by an individual, you must ensure these are documented in a care plan and communicated to other staff including visiting professionals.

The main reason for *not* carrying out a task that you have not been trained to do is that you might do more harm to the person concerned.

You are accountable for your actions, so make sure that you are trained and feel competent to do a task.

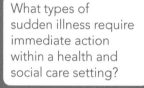

think about

Why do you think emergency first aid tasks should only be carried out by qualified first aiders?

think about

What types of sudden illness require immediate action within a health and social care setting?

8.4 Reducing the spread of infection

How an infection can get into the body

From time to time everyone suffers from infections and these may be bacterial or viral.

Bacteria and viruses enter the body through:

- the respiratory tract (breathing in contaminated particles)
- breaks in the skin (caused by bites, stings, injections, fractures, cuts and grazes)

Infections spread easily

the digestive tract (consuming contaminated food and drink)

the reproductive and urinary tract (infections of the uterus, anus, bladder or kidneys).

find out!

Contagious
A disease that is spread by physical contact.

Key Term

Looking at the routes of infection, what is the most likely cause of a **contagious** spread of infection?
How can this be easily spread or transmitted?

How your own health and hygiene might pose a risk

It is important to go to work feeling well enough to do your job and not carrying an infection. You may be able to fight it off, but people who are older or unwell are vulnerable and are not able to fight off infections so easily.

If you have a cold, cough or high temperature you should not work where you will be in contact with vulnerable people. Similarly, you should stay away from work if you have a stomach bug (diarrhoea and/or vomiting).

Remember also that if you do not practise good hygiene, then you put the people in your care at risk of infections from bacteria on your hands. You should cover any cuts with a waterproof dressing.

think about

List the times when you must thoroughly wash your hands during the course of a shift in the health and care sector.

Steps for thorough hand washing

Washing your hands regularly and thoroughly for 15–20 seconds will help minimise possible infections. The Department of Health recommends a five-step procedure for effective hand washing:

1. Wet hands.

2. Apply soap thoroughly.

3. Lather and scrub (including in between fingers, nails, fingertips, back and front of hands).

4. Rinse thoroughly.

5. Dry thoroughly using a paper towel or an air dryer.

Simple diagrams of handwashing routines can be found by typing 'hand washing diagrams' into the internet.

Personal protective equipment

Pathogenic bacteria could be anywhere within a health and social care setting. If you do not handle potentially contaminated objects carefully, you risk transmitting bacteria to vulnerable individuals in your care or to colleagues or visitors.

> **Pathogenic bacteria** Harmful bacteria that can make people ill if transmitted.
>
> **Key Term**

think about

What do you think are possible 'contaminated objects' in health and social care?

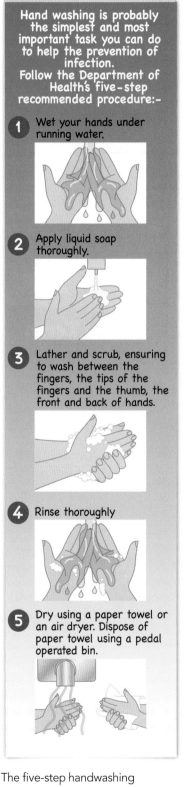

Hand washing is probably the simplest and most important task you can do to help the prevention of infection.
Follow the Department of Health's five-step recommended procedure:-

1. Wet your hands under running water.

2. Apply liquid soap thoroughly.

3. Lather and scrub, ensuring to wash between the fingers, the tips of the fingers and the thumb, the front and back of hands.

4. Rinse thoroughly

5. Dry using a paper towel or an air dryer. Dispose of paper towel using a pedal operated bin.

The five-step handwashing procedure

Case study

In Practice

PPE The acronym for 'Personal Protective Equipment'. It is anything that creates a barrier between the worker and possible contamination. Examples are: disposable gloves and aprons; caps, nets or hats for food handlers.

Key Term

Shahina is shown how to wear **PPE** (personal protective equipment) when changing beds, especially soiled beds. She still needs to wash her hands before and after each task. When it is time to assist with the medication round, she checks that the residents' hands are clean before they receive their tablets. She is also shown how to practise not actually touching the tablets.

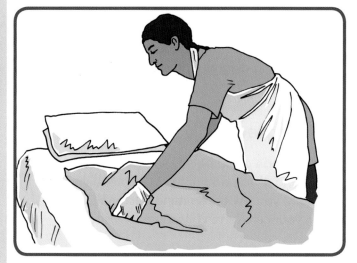

Always wear PPE when you need to

As Shahina then assists with afternoon tea and cakes, she makes sure she washes her hands before this task, checks residents' hands again and removes old food as soon as possible.

What would you do?

When soiled sheets and any clinical items such as dirty dressings are removed, what do you think is meant by 'safe and hygienic waste disposal?' Describe what you would do.

8.5 Moving and handling equipment and other objects safely

Legislation that relates to moving and handling

Remember that the Health and Safety at Work Act (1974) sets out responsibilities for the employer and the employee to keep themselves safe by following agreed procedures.

The Manual Handling Operations Regulations (1992) set out a series of steps that organisations should follow.

If the lifting or manoeuvre must be carried out, you should assess the risk of injury using TILE:

T = the **task**: what does this involve doing in terms of bending or twisting or lifting?

I = the **individual**: what is their weight and their general health?

L = load: is the person difficult to grip and handle and what equipment may be needed?

E = environment: consider the space, any slippery surfaces and the 'end' place where you want to be.

Some related legislation is the Management of Health and Safety at Work Regulations (1999). These set out the legal requirements for all potentially unsafe activities – these must be checked before they are carried out, using formal 'risk assessments'. Remember the five steps for risk assessing (see page 136).

did you know?

It is recommended that you should avoid all tasks which may involve the risk of injury.

The principles for safe moving and handling

As well as following the TILE and risk assessment steps given on page 143, you must make sure your lifting techniques are not going to strain your body. The following are very basic principles and you are strongly advised to seek specialist training:

1. Keep the person (or load) close to you.

2. Avoid any twisting.

3. Keep your balance by standing with feet shoulder-width apart.

4. Bend your knees, not your waist, and keep your head and spine in alignment.

In Practice

For each scenario in the table below, use TILE and the risk assessment steps to show your understanding of preventing injury when manual handling. Copy the table and write your answers to the questions.

Scenario	TILE steps	Risk assessment steps
Brent is 21 stone, short of breath and unable to bear weight. He needs transferring to a wheelchair from his bed to go to the toilet.	1 Bending, twisting or lifting? 2 What are the concerns re the individual? 3 How might the load be difficult? 4 What possible constraints are there?	1 What is the risk of injury? 2 Who might be harmed? 3 How might the risk be reduced? 4 What will need to be recorded? 5 When and why a review?
Mrs Cooper is a frail 94-year-old. She is unsteady on her feet but would like to take a bath.	1 Bending, twisting or lifting? 2 What are the concerns re the individual? 3 How might the load be difficult? 4 What possible constraints are there?	1 What is the risk of injury? 2 Who might be harmed? 3 How might the risk be reduced? 4 What will need to be recorded? 5 When and why a review?

Why moving and handling tasks should only be carried out after specialist training

Specialist training is required because, as is the case with first aid procedures, if you try to do a task for which you are not trained you could endanger the individual, yourself or other people. There are special techniques for moving your body in certain ways to avoid stress on the muscles and the skeleton. Damage to these areas can cause long-term disabilities.

You are accountable as a care worker for your actions and so must make sure you are properly trained and assessed as competent before you agree to do anything. Your manager will confirm that you are competent during supervision sessions.

However, if you do not feel confident you must always say so. Your manager or mentor will arrange for further work shadowing or for more work experience.

8.6 The principles of assisting and moving an individual

Although individuals and loads have been mentioned already, there are some particular factors to consider when moving people as opposed to loads.

find out!

What do you think the 'other factors' you need to consider are when moving people in a care setting?

Look at www.nhs.uk and search for 'lifting techniques'.

Case study

In Practice

Assess the risks, consult the plan and check the ability of an individual before carrying out the transfer

Shahina is asked to assist with transferring Mrs Collins, an 89-year-old partially sighted woman, from her bed to a chair. The available space and the environment have been assessed for safety.

Aware of the importance of effective communication, Shahina seeks consent from Mrs Collins to move her – explaining why she is to be moved and how she will be moved. Once Mrs Collins has given her consent, Shahina prepares for the task – slowly assessing the strength and ability of the lady to ease herself to the edge of the bed and keeping her own body close. She has consulted a care plan that states that Mrs Collins is able to do this and to stand unaided for a short time. Shahina is fitting the task to the person. This is called **ergonomics**.

Case study

In Practice

Ergonomics
Fitting a task to the individual, their capabilities, strength, stability and mental capacity. It can involve the use of aids.

Key Term

Shahina has to bring a hoist for Mrs Cooper, a 94-year-old woman who would like to take a bath. She has been instructed to check the parts of the mobile hoist for safety and to check the handling care plan. She needs the assistance of a second person. She obtains consent, conducts a risk assessment of Mrs Cooper's condition and prepares items for the bath. The two carers work as a team to carefully lift Mrs Cooper, using the appropriate slings correctly and smoothly so there is no friction on her skin. They explain to her all the movements and check if she feels comfortable.

There are many types of mechanical aids available and it is important that you are trained to use the types that are in use in your setting.

In the 'Find Out' activity on page 145, you considered other factors to think about when moving people in a care setting. Your answers should have included: dignity, respect, effective communication and promoting independence. The lady that Shahina is transferring to a chair, Mrs Collins, will appreciate being told where she is going and how she will be moved because her vision is poor; but all individuals who are unable to move themselves need to be given this information.

People who are moved and handled by others feel a loss of control and need to feel they can trust their carers.

This will definitely be the case for the individual who Shahina is transferring into the bath, Mrs Cooper, because at 94 she is very frail.

There are also physical factors to consider. These include the condition of the person's skin and any medical conditions that may be affected by moving. Skin may be broken, sore or fragile, in which case sudden movement or friction will worsen the condition.

If an individual is short of breath, you may have to consider the use of inhalers if prescribed or stopping and allowing the person time to rest between each stage of the manoeuvre.

If they have not received specialist training, carers may not be able to fully assess a situation and they could harm individuals or themselves.

find out!

What types of mechanical aids, equipment and materials are available in your setting? Check that you are fully trained to use them and look at the handling care plan.

Following an individual's care plan

As you have seen with the case studies on page 146, each person has a care plan to follow that allows as much independence and choice as possible. It is a legal requirement to obtain valid consent and to assess any possible risks that a procedure may involve. If an individual refuses to be moved, then you must not carry out this process.

Care plans can change because an individual's circumstances may change. If a person's skin condition gets worse, or their health deteriorates in any way, then their ability to participate and engage in moving procedures also becomes more difficult. Reviews are therefore essential in order to maintain the level of support that the individual needs.

8.7 Handling hazardous substances

The Control of Substances Hazardous to Health (COSHH) Regulations (2002) set out requirements for employers to prevent or control exposure to any substance that may cause harm.

These substances include cleaning fluids, corrosives (which contain acid), flammable substances (solvents), clinical waste (which contain some biological agents), used needles (contaminated with blood), soiled dressings (contaminated with blood and body fluid) and any bodily fluids (blood, faeces, vomit, sputum). They also include medicines, oral medications, liquid medications and preparations for injection into the body.

Hazard symbol	Hazard classification
T+ or T	**Very Toxic (T+) / Toxic (T)** Chemicals which in very low quantities cause death or acute or chronic damage to health when inhaled, swallowed or absorbed through the skin.
Xn	**Harmful** Chemicals which may cause death or acute or chronic damage to health.
C	**Corrosive** Chemicals which on contact with living tissues may destroy them.
Xi	**Irritant** Non-corrosive chemicals which through immediate, prolonged or repeated contact with the skin or mucous membranes, may cause inflammation.
E	**Explosive** Chemicals that may react producing heat without atmospheric oxygen, quickly producing gases, and which can detonate and explode.
O	**Oxidising** Chemicals which give rise to heat-producing reactions when in contact with other substances, particularly flammable substances.

Table of hazard classifications

Hazard symbol	Hazard classification
F+ or F	**Flammable** **Extremely (F+)**: Liquids that have an extremely low flash point (below 0°C) and low boiling point (equal to or below 35°C). Or gaseous substances which are flammable in contact with air at ambient temperature and pressure. **Highly (F)**: Chemicals which may become hot and catch fire in contact with air at ambient temperature without any application of energy. A solid which readily catches fire with minimal contact with a source of ignition and which continues to burn after the source is removed. Liquids with a very low flash point (equal to or less than 21°C) that are not classified as extremely flammable. *(Flash point is the lowest temperature at which a liquid can ignite in the air. Ambient temperature is the temperature of the surroundings.)*

Table of hazard classifications

Storing hazardous substances

It is important to follow the manufacturer's guidelines for safe storage. Some items should not be stored near others and you must note any incompatibility. Your setting will also have guidelines for storing hazardous substances and you must follow these carefully.

Using hazardous substances

If you are carrying out any cleaning activities, it is important to read the instructions on the label of the cleaning substance.

- Dilution strength varies with different products and you must dilute according to the instructions.

- You may be required to use PPE, for example to wear disposable gloves and aprons. You should never inhale fumes or get the substance near your eyes.

- Always wash your hands afterwards – even if you wore gloves.

- Good practice also requires you to seal off the area if you are cleaning, particularly if it is the floor. Floors should not be walked on until they are completely dry and non-slippery.

The basic principles for administering medication are covered on page 156.

find out!

What types of hazardous substances can you identify in your setting and how are they stored?

Disposing of hazardous substances

Safe disposal is also part of the essential standard for the handling of medications. Records of disposal are kept as a legal requirement and this includes controlled drugs. This is because they can be abused if they fall into the wrong hands. They may also harm the environment.

You must put used needles into a sharps box, which should never be more than two-thirds full when sealed. You should never pour liquids down the sink. Along with other medications that are no longer required, they should be returned to the pharmacy.

Ensure sharps containers are only two-thirds full

Never pour liquid medicines down a sink or toilet

Organisations that produce clinical waste, such as dressings from a nursing home as opposed to a personal and residential care home, must register with a licensed waste disposal company that can treat potentially hazardous biological waste. You should place this kind of waste is placed in yellow clinical bags.

Good hygiene is essential when carrying out safe disposal. You must use gloves and aprons and you should also wash your hands afterwards and before doing any other task.

8.8 Environmental safety procedures in the social care setting

Fire prevention

It is a legal requirement for all workplaces to clearly display the actions required in the event of a fire. The Regulatory Reform (Fire Safety) Order (2005) sets out the principles for risk assessments and prevention of fires:

- All workplaces should keep fire doors closed and free from clutter.

- Smoke alarms should be in working order.

- Staff should attend fire lectures once a year and be aware of the extinguishers on site and how to use them.

- Electrical items are tested once a year and residents and visitors are not allowed to smoke on the premises.

What to do in the event of a fire

The basic procedure in the event of a fire is:

1. Raise the alarm.

2. Dial 999.

3. Prepare for evacuation to the assembly point.

4. If possible, use the correct extinguisher on a small fire.

5. Check the number and names of people assembled using registers.

6. Do not return to the building until a fire officer gives permission.

It is your duty to reduce the risk of fire (for example, by not leaving pans unattended), to know where the equipment is, to keep fire exits clear and to know how to operate extinguishers if necessary. Fire training is part of your induction training.

Gas leak prevention

The manager should ensure that gas appliances are checked at least once a year.

You must familiarise yourself with the procedure in the event of a gas leak and learn to recognise suspicious smells, such as gas. You should reduce the risk of a gas leak by turning off gas appliances when you have finished using them.

Emergency numbers should be displayed in your workplace. It is important to evacuate in the same way as for a fire, helping those with mobility problems and guiding others who are mobile. You will need to make sure there are no naked flames or inflammable liquids in the vicinity. Do not return to the building until it is safe.

Floods

Remember that you should always turn off taps when you have finished using them. If there is a flood, try to stop water from entering rooms. If you are able to evacuate safely, then you must do so – following the guidelines of the setting. Electrical appliances are a potential hazard in the event of a flood; if equipment is in use it must be turned off if water is likely to come into contact with the current.

Intruders and preventing security breaches

The security of a home is essential and there are ways to ensure this is maintained:

- All staff and visiting personnel must wear identification badges

- Use of security codes on external doors and perhaps staff carrying a fob for internal doors

- Safety locks on windows and doors

- Security personnel, especially at night

- Maintenance of alarm systems.

You must report anyone on the premises who looks suspicious. Prevention is safer than allowing people free access. It is important to ask visitors to sign a book and to indicate who they have come to see. Obtaining permission from the resident before allowing a visitor to see them is good practice. Any refusals should be respected.

You should never confront a stranger, but do call for help and, if any violence or disruption occurs, call the police.

8.9 **Managing stress**

Common signs and indicators of stress

If you are suffering from stress, and things seem to get too much for you, your body will struggle physically. Sometimes this means you do not sleep well or eat well. Alternatively, you might overeat or drink too much alcohol. You may become grumpy, irritable and bad-tempered or timid, tearful and not wanting to socialise. Some people develop habits like biting their nails, while others may be unable to concentrate or start forgetting things.

If someone knows you well, they can usually identify the signs and symptoms of stress. However, new colleagues, visitors and residents will not recognise the signs and they may react negatively, which can make you feel even worse. Eventually you may lose your self-esteem and feelings of self-worth, and may label yourself as 'useless'.

The worst case scenario is when you feel it is not worth getting up in the morning, washing or looking after yourself properly and as a result your health suffers.

What circumstances tend to trigger your own stress?

It is important to maintain a healthy outlook and a positive attitude, but everyone can find this difficult sometimes. Recognising when you are feeling low is a crucial early step in doing something about it.

Different things upset different people. It is often hard to accept that things may not be as serious as you think and to look at the 'bigger picture'. It is natural to experience some 'pain' about a negative opinion or a criticism at work, but it is dangerous to dwell on these thoughts.

If you feel you are unable to cope with the demands of your job or do not want to be there, your feelings will just get worse.

Sometimes home life does not fit in with the demands of a job, for example if there is illness in the family, a bad relationship or money worries. This can lead to feeling a loss of control that spills over into your other roles. It is important to try to identify the **stressors** that affect you so you can manage these quickly.

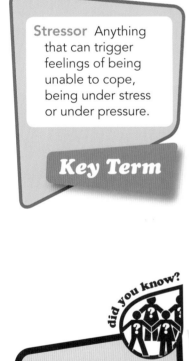

Stressor Anything that can trigger feelings of being unable to cope, being under stress or under pressure.

Key Term

According to the mental health charity MIND every year over 5 million people have time off due to mental pressures at work.

Ways of managing stress

Acknowledging you are under pressure is an important first step. You must talk about these feelings with your mentor, line manager or employer. Don't be afraid to ask for a few minutes of their time; they are there to support you.

It is a good idea to think about why you might be feeling the way that you do. It could be that you dislike someone you work with or that you feel you cannot manage a certain individual or a particular task. You might have problems balancing your work life with your home life and cannot see a solution.

Talking to colleagues and your team leader, mentor or manager may give you some 'managing options', such as suggestions for changing the work role, working elsewhere, different shift patterns or fewer hours.

Extra training may help to tackle feelings of inadequacy or attending a course may improve your self-esteem. But you should avoid drinking too much alcohol or smoking more cigarettes; these actions are temporary releases and won't resolve your problems – they will just lead to others.

Ideas for relaxing as a release from stress can include having a massage, visiting a spa, getting some fresh air and exercise, talking with friends or going out for a meal or to see a film. You might like painting, singing, playing an instrument or listening to music. Some people refer to these types of activities as 'escapism', but this is a good thing if it stops you feeling under pressure.

Over-indulgence does not solve your problems

8.10 Procedures for handling medication

Procedures for handling medication are set out in *The Handling of Medicines in Social Care* (2007) (Royal Pharmaceutical Society). These guidelines set out eight key principles for care providers to follow. Principle 3 is that:

'Care staff who help people with their medicine are competent' before administering medication. For more information, visit: www.rpharms.com/social-care-settings-pdfs/the-handling-of-medicines-in-social-care.pdf

Safe handling of medicines depends on the type of medication and how it is administered. You should ask your manager if you can do a 'Safe Handling of Medicines' course.

Never leave a medication trolley unattended

You should quickly familiarise yourself with:
- your individuals' medicines, what they are and what they are for
- the route of the medication and the usual dose and strength
- how to monitor the effects, and whether these are beneficial or not
- how to recognise a serious side effect and what to do if this happens.

The Handling of Medicines in Social Care also sets out guidelines for ordering, storing, administering and disposing of medications. All procedures involve recording and the signatures of key people who handle medication. There are strict rules for storing medication. Some drugs are addictive and might be dangerous in the wrong hands. These drugs are referred to as 'controlled drugs', as they must be stored separately in a locked cabinet within a locked cupboard and the amounts used have to be counted and recorded in a special book. When the cabinet is opened it triggers a red light which shows that the controlled drugs cabinet is in use.

A second person must witness the administering of any controlled drug and countersign the amount given and the amount remaining. One of these people must be qualified to administer controlled drugs.

Other drugs are kept in a locked cupboard or in a locked trolley, which must not be left unattended.

Some medications such as eye drops and certain antibiotics must be stored in a lockable fridge (which is used for the purpose of storing medications only).

Basic principles for administering medication are:

- to obtain the individual's consent to receive the medication

- to wash your hands first and ensure the good hygiene of the individual receiving the medication – using a non-touch technique is good practice

- to identify the correct medication, dosage, strength, time and route for the correct patient

- to use the MAR (medicine administration record) sheet to initial the medications given (ensure that the medications are actually taken by the individual)

- to monitor any effects of the medication.

Who is responsible for medication in a social care setting?

The person with the overall responsibility for medication is the registered person (usually the employer or manager). However, they might delegate responsibility to a deputy or a 'designated officer'. This person will keep possession of the keys to medication.

It is important to realise that medications are the property of the person for whom they are prescribed and every encouragement should be given to individuals to manage their own medications and be self-administrators. However, this may be hazardous and you need to consider why.

> ### What would you do?
>
> If an individual wants to take their own medication, which consists of potentially dangerous controlled drugs, what risk factors need to be considered? To help you, visit:
>
> www.rpharms.com/social-care-settings-pdfs/the-handling-of-medicines-in-social-care.pdf
>
> This is a document called *The Handling of Medicines in Social Care* (2007) that provides excellent guidance.

> Regulation 13 of the Essential Standards of Quality and Safety (Health and Social Care Act 2008) states: 'The registered person must protect individuals against the risks associated with the unsafe use and management of medicines, by making appropriate arrangements for the obtaining, recording, handling, using, safe keeping, dispensing, safe administration and disposal of medicines.'
> The associated outcome is Outcome 9: 'People have their medicines when they need them and in a safe way. People are given information about their medicines.'

Medication must only be handled following specialist training

If no training in medication was given to care staff, all kinds of dangerous errors could happen. For example:

- individuals could be given the wrong medication or too much medication
- medicines might not be stored securely
- adverse effects might not get reported
- special instructions for administering medication might not be followed, which could have harmful effects on an individual.

It is very important, as well as being a legal requirement, that training is given to care workers. This includes having the correct knowledge and understanding as well as demonstrating competence when storing, administering, recording and disposing of medication.

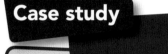

Case study

In Practice

Shahina has just completed a 'Safe Handling of Medicines' course and has assisted the senior care worker with a medicine round. She will not do this by herself until the manager has assessed her as competent, confident and able.

find out!

What is the difference between Level 1, Level 2 and Level 3 training in handling medicines?

What would you do?

Your organisation must have procedures in place in the event of the following:

1 Someone refuses their medication.
2 You notice mental or physical changes to the person.
3 Someone tells you that the tablet you are about to give them has already been given.

Describe what you would do in each case.

8.11 How to handle and store food safely

Food safety standards

The Food Safety Act (1990) states that you are in breach of the law if you sell or serve food that is unfit for eating and likely to make people ill.

The Food Hygiene (England) Regulations (2006) are mainly concerned with temperature control (following strict guidelines on cooking to correct temperatures to kill off any pathogenic bacteria).

Regulation (EC) 852/2004 on the hygiene of foodstuffs sets out standards of acceptable hygiene on premises, including the hygiene of handlers, equipment used and training requirements.

If a complaint is investigated and it is discovered that people have been made ill by poor hygiene, poor temperature regulation or not adhering to standards, there are severe penalties such as prison or heavy fines for those concerned.

Storage of food

You should be aware of the correct requirements for storing food, as incorrect storage could lead to food poisoning.

Food is purchased with a 'use by' date or a 'best before' date. It is a legal requirement to stick to these dates when serving food to the public.

think about

Why do some foods display a 'best before' date and others a 'use by' date?

What are the correct fridge and freezer temperatures that must be maintained in a setting?
Find out the meaning of 'hot holding' when referring to just-cooked food.

Certain principles and procedures must be followed when storing food:

- Food is best put away as soon as possible after delivery.

- Food that is chilled should remain chilled and placed in a refrigerator.

- Food that is frozen should be placed in the freezer (unless the food is being defrosted), then placed in the bottom of the fridge and covered.

- Cold cooked foods should be stored on a higher shelf in the fridge well away from uncooked raw foods.

- Cooked and uncooked meats should not be stored together.

- Just-cooked food that is still hot must not be stored in a fridge and once cold can only be reheated once (to the correct temperature).

- All food should be covered.

- Food that may cause allergies such as nuts and seeds must be stored separately in airtight containers.

Maximise hygiene when handling food

The most important task when you are about to handle food is correct hand washing (see page 141). If you are dealing with raw food and cooked food, it is essential that you wash your hands in between handling each type and that you keep them separate.

Your setting will use PPE (personal protective equipment), for food handling, which may include hats, disposable gloves and aprons.

If you have a cut on your hand or fingers, you must cover it with a blue waterproof plaster when handling food. The waterproof element is a legal requirement.

Your equipment and utensils should also be scrupulously clean, including probes that are used to check **core temperatures** of meat.

Core temperature
The temperature of the thickest part of the meat, for example, in between the breast and leg of whole chicken.

Key Term

Tasks performed in a kitchen must be carried out separately, for example preparing raw meat away from the preparation of cooked food (including sandwiches). If the same person performs both tasks, then scrupulous hand washing is essential, together with the use of separate chopping boards and utensils. Ideally you would prepare sandwiches first for chilled storage.

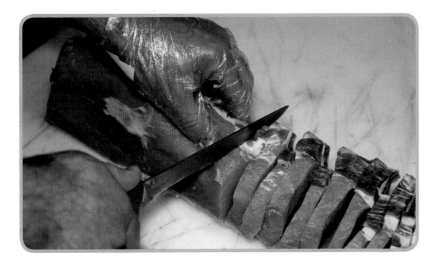

The highest standards of hygiene are essential in food preparation

How to dispose of food

You should always work from clean areas to 'dirty areas' and clean up as you go, instead of allowing a mess to accumulate. waste food. You must dispose of waste food as soon as possible into bins with tight-fitting lids, separating wet waste from dry waste.

What would you do?

You are asked to help the cook put away the deliveries, which contain fresh cooked beef, raw fish and some raw chicken. There are also some eggs, cheese, cakes and scones and butter.

List six tasks that you would do that would demonstrate your knowledge of food hygiene.

think about

What are the hazards of not disposing of food properly?

Common hazards when handling and storing food

If you do not stick to high standards when handling food, there are a number of hazards that could occur.

Copy the table below. Then read the statements and place a tick in the correct column

Food handling task	True	False
You check that the temperature of the fridge is no more than 8 degrees.		
You store raw food at the top of the fridge, covered.		
You wash your hands before and after serving lunch.		
You can reheat a cooked lasagne for a resident until is warm enough to eat without scalding her.		
It is acceptable for a guide dog to be allowed in the kitchen as long as you do not stroke it.		

Quick Quiz

1   If you did not carry out a risk assessment you would be in breach of:
    a. The Health and Safety at Work Act (1974)
    b. The Management of Health and Safety at Work Regulations (1999)
    c. COSHH (2002)
    d. RIDDOR (1995).

2   The COSHH (Control of Substances Hazardous to Health) Regulations address:
    a. the disposal of medicines
    b. the dilution of cleaning materials
    c. discarding soiled items
    d. all of these.

3   A care worker signs a contract to:
    a. agree to work to the organisation's policies and procedures
    b. get promoted
    c. deliver their own ideas on care values
    d. work with a team leader.

4   Which of the following is an example of a hazard?
    a. A risk of a pan boiling over.
    b. Spillage of blood on the floor.
    c. Bees outside an open window.
    d. A spider's web in a resident's room.

5   Between attending to individuals it is best practice to:
    a. record entries in the care plan
    b. change your uniform
    c. wash your hands
    d. report to your manager.

6   For emergency first aid the advised CPR rate (for adults) is currently:
    a. 60 compressions to 2 breaths
    b. 20 compressions to 5 breaths
    c. 40 compressions to 2 breaths
    d. 30 compressions to 2 breaths.

7   Because controlled drugs are addictive and potentially dangerous, they must be:
    a. placed in a communal area
    b. only sold in quantities of five per packet
    c. stored securely following strict regulations
    d. dispensed only by the manager.

8   Fire regulations state that there must be:
    a. paper storage only at the back of a room
    b. one fire blanket per building
    c. fire extinguishers and notices of the evacuation procedure
    d. a fire officer on duty at night.

9   Before moving anyone manually, you must check:
    a. the care plan
    b. the person gives consent
    c. the environment
    d. all of the above.

10 A high risk to food safety is:
    a. a beef pie cooked until piping hot
    b. a salad chilled and in date
    c. thawing chicken at the bottom of the fridge overnight
    d. storing yoghurts at 10 degrees in the fridge.

Unit 9

Understand how to
handle information
in
social care settings

This unit introduces you to the process of recording, storing and sharing information in social care settings. When you work in social care settings you have to handle lots of different types of information about the clients you assist and support. Some of it will be spoken information and some of it will be written. A lot of the information that you deal with will be confidential. The unit focuses on the need for sensitive handling of information relating to clients, introducing you to the correct methods of processing information and outlining the associated policies and laws.

On completion of this unit you should:

- understand the need for secure handling of information in social care settings

- know how to access support for handling information in social care settings.

9.1 Handling information securely in social care settings

Processing different types of information correctly

As a social care worker you will be dealing with different types of information on a daily basis. You will need to receive written and spoken information, record it, store it, pass it on and sometimes dispose of it. You must carry out each stage of this process correctly.

did you know?

Care notes and support plans are legal documents that may need to be referred to in a court of law. You must always write in pen and never erase, scribble over or 'white out' what has been written. Instead, draw through mistakes with a single line and initial it (so you can be traced for clarification), then rewrite what you meant to record.

It is important to handle information correctly

Tip

REED
SOCIAL CARE
●●●

In social care, it is essential to be able to record information accurately and succinctly. You can demonstrate your ability to do this to a prospective employer by ensuring that your CV is well-written, neat, organised and spelt correctly. Ask a friend or family member to double check your CV before you send it off to prospective employers.

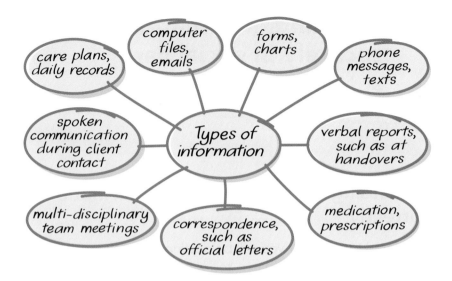

Different types of information in a health and social care setting

How to identify, record and store information correctly

At work you will need to identify information that is relevant before recording it accurately and storing it safely on:

- paper
- computers
- smartphones or electronic notebooks
- portable devices, such as a memory stick.

Information must be securely recorded and stored, and disposed of appropriately when it is no longer needed. If information about people is not handled correctly, it could be seen by people who should not see it or it might be damaged, stolen or lost. This may have serious consequences.

Ask a senior colleague how long personal records about clients must be retained in your work setting. Then find out the measures taken to make sure they are completed correctly, kept securely and later disposed of safely.

Source of information	Correct recording and storage
Handwritten records	Handwriting must be legible. Record factual information only. Write up notes promptly. Sign and date what you write
Personal files	Label client files clearly to prevent mix-ups. Keep confidential files in a locked cabinet, with access restricted to named staff. In a client's own home, agree with colleagues and clients where to keep notes safe. Make sure you know the correct procedure for accessing files. from their storage place.
Computer files and emails	Use client initials rather than names in emails or other 'public' communications. Use Encrypted files/emails or passwords to access work computers. *Never* give anyone else your password. *Never* use another person's password.
Telephone calls	Follow an agreed system for taking phone messages. Dispose of rough notes securely, by shredding, as soon as a message is passed on.
Face-to-face communication	If you are not the correct person to receive a message, request minimum information to pass on to the relevant person. Decide if information needs to be recorded as well as passed on verbally. Make sure you record names and take contact details when receiving information from individuals outside your organisation.

Ways of recording and storing information

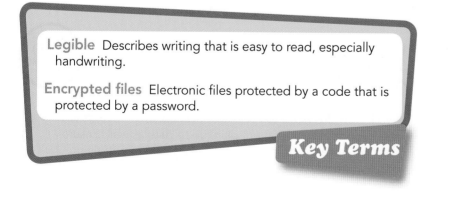

Legible Describes writing that is easy to read, especially handwriting.

Encrypted files Electronic files protected by a code that is protected by a password.

Key Terms

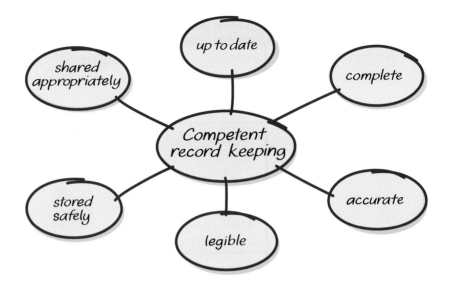

The six principles of competent record keeping

Keeping records up to date

Tasks such as writing in someone's care file, recording medication given and making notes about conversations should be done as soon as possible after you have carried out the activities, so that you do not forget essential information. On some records, such as medication charts, you need to record the time as well as signing and dating the chart. Make sure that any information from outside the workplace, such as professional reports, gets filed in accordance with your organisation's record keeping system, making everything easy to find. Regularly check with clients (or their relatives) whether contact information (address, email, telephone numbers) is up to date.

Tip

REED
SOCIAL CARE
•••

Just as it is important to keep all records up to date while at work, you also need to keep your own personal records (CV and personal development plan) up to date as well. Ensure that you take the time to add new skills gained or training you have undertaken to your CV and PDP so that you are always marketing yourself in the most effective way when looking for a new position.

Case study

In Practice

Younis is having a hectic shift at the care home. He has been asked to encourage one resident who has a urinary tract infection to drink more and he has a fluid intake chart to complete, as well as a number of residents to weigh. One resident complains of indigestion, which goes away when he gives her peppermint tea, but another requires tablets for her pain. Younis is carrying a great deal of information in his head and just hopes he will remember it all when it comes to writing up the daily notes.

1. What do you recommend Younis does to make sure he remembers all the information correctly?

2. What different types of records will Younis need to complete?

3. Identify two things Younis needs to do to record and store information correctly.

Ensuring records are accurate

As well as being kept up to date and complete, the details of any records must be correct, especially who said or did what. Only record what you have done yourself, and sign only for yourself. If a senior staff member asks you to record something on their behalf, make this clear in what you write. Always, say where you got the information from. For example, if a family member asks you to put something in a client's file, record their name and make it clear that you are quoting information supplied by someone other than yourself. Finally, be careful when recording numbers and quantities, especially when administering prescribed drugs or dealing with money.

Key Term

Abbreviations
Shortened forms of words or phrases; for example, 'meds' for 'medicines', or ENT for 'Ear, Nose and Throat'.

Keeping records legible and easy to understand

Your own handwriting must be clear and easy to read. Write in clear, simple sentences. Do not use abbreviations unless a manager has said this is all right. Always check that your spellings are correct. Do not rely on computer spell-checkers; these often use American spellings and may not recognise the correct spelling of surnames or specialist words used in your work setting.

Ensuring records are stored safely

You should always put files, or other paperwork, back as soon as you have used them. Check that files are stored in accordance with your organisation's filing system. If you are allowed to unlock a cabinet, lock it again as soon as possible, and immediately return the key. Do not allow members of the public (including relatives) to be in record storage rooms unsupervised. If using files or records on the computer, change your password as often as you can, and do not let anyone else use it. When working on a computer, make sure that you regularly save the document, and ask senior staff about how to back up information on the computer. If you use a smartphone or laptop away from the office, make sure you keep it with you at all times.

Your questions answered

What should I do if a client's record is incomplete?

Make sure you know the rules in your workplace about when and how often you need to record something in a client's file. Clients' records are legal documents, so you will be held legally accountable for what you write in them. If a record is incomplete, *never* make up information to fill the gap. Instead, tell a senior member of staff immediately. You may be asked to contact other people who were present in order to complete the record accurately.

Sharing information appropriately

Information must only be given to those who really need to know it. It is equally important to make sure that information is passed on when it is needed. This includes information you have gained from clients about their needs or preferences, especially if these have changed. Colleagues or visiting practitioners may need information about a client, especially if the person has communication difficulties. If you are worried about any change in an individual, report it privately, away from the hearing of the client and others. In the same way, you should record any new information about a person – provided, for example, by a district nurse – and share it with a senior member of staff. Always share and record information in an **objective** way that avoids criticising, judging or demeaning the individual.

Objective
Describing something in a purely factual, non-emotional way.

Key Term

Tip

REED
SOCIAL CARE

When sharing information via your CV when applying for a new job, you need to keep this information relevant to each position that you apply for. It is better to tailor your CV slightly for each position that you apply for, rather than having a 'one size fits all' CV, which could lead to your prospective employer reading a lot of irrelevant information.

Case study

In Practice

Jon works in a home for young adults with learning disabilities. Three residents have a fight one morning. Nobody is hurt, but Jon is asked to complete an incident form. He discusses this with a colleague while assisting residents to eat lunch and, between the two of them, they try to work out who was to blame for the fight so that Jon can complete the form accurately.

1. Why should Jon not have discussed the incident with the clients present during lunch?

2. What information do you think was relevant to include in the incident report?

It is important to record incidents as soon as possible

Recognise confidential information and know how to manage it securely

Social care workers need to know personal information about their clients in order to provide appropriate support and assistance, for example details about their family and their life. You will probably need to share information like this with other practitioners, such as social workers.

Some of this information will be confidential and you must know how to deal with this in a professional way. Remember, you must not share information outside the workplace about the people you care for, even if you do not use their name. It is *never* OK to gossip at or about your work. You must also make sure that confidential information is not overheard or seen by the wrong people.

Confidentiality does not mean keeping things secret. It means making sure that only people who need to know or have a right to know **confidential information** have access to it. Social care organisations will have a written confidentiality policy that will set out procedures for the correct ways to handle confidential information. Make sure you read this, understand it and know how it applies to your everyday work.

Confidentiality
The process of recognising certain information as sensitive, keeping it secure and only sharing it with those who need to know in order to provide care and support.

Confidential information
Information that may only be accessed by individuals who have the authority or permission to access it.

Key Terms

find out!

Ask to see the confidentiality policy at your place of work. Take time to read it carefully, making notes about the aspects that directly affect your working practice. Ask a senior colleague or your supervisor about anything you don't understand.

How do you know if information is confidential?

The different types of information you will be expected to handle that are confidential may concern:

- physical and mental health status and history

- personal details to do with identity, such as religion and sexual orientation

- physical measurements, such as weight and height

- test and investigation results, such as blood and urine tests and x-rays

- family information about relationships and personal history

- financial and legal matters.

When must confidentiality be broken?

Occasionally, the normal rules about confidentiality must be broken. This happens when the need to protect a client, or to protect others, is more important than the need to keep information private. Examples of people who you might need to share confidential information with are the police or a doctor, who needs to know the information in order to keep the person safe and healthy. Times when you need to break confidentiality include when:

- a person is at risk of harm, such as showing suicidal behaviour

- a person has committed, or is about to commit, a crime

- the health or safety of others is at risk

- abuse of a child or adult is disclosed or suspected

- a court orders certain information to be disclosed.

Legislation relating to recording, storing and sharing information

Handling information is such an important area of social care practice that there are laws about it. The law can be complicated, but don't worry, you are not expected to be an expert! Remember that the law affects all kinds of information and does not refer only to written information.

What would you do?

Lindsey hasn't been a carer for long when she begins visiting Mrs Forster, who has dementia and has just been diagnosed with breast cancer. When Lindsey is pegging out washing, a neighbour calls to her over the fence to ask about Mrs Forster. Lindsey comments on how unfair it is that as well as having dementia she now faces cancer too. She adds that Mrs Forster is 'made of tough stuff' though and 'won't give in to illness without a fight'.

- What information is acceptable and unacceptable for Lindsey to share with the neighbour?
- How would you reply to the neighbour if you were Lindsey?

What do you need to know about the law?

The main legislation affecting the recording, storage and sharing of information is outlined in the table below.

Legislation	What does it say?
Data Protection Act (1998)	Information should be: • used in ways that are fair, keep to the law and uphold a person's rights • recorded accurately, limited to what is required and used only for the purpose you have stated • transferred/shared with others in ways that take proper precautions to keep it safe • stored in ways that are secure and kept no longer than is necessary
Human Rights Act (1998)	Even if a person is in care, or can no longer give their consent for information about them to be shared, you must make sure their privacy is respected.
Freedom of Information Act (2000)	Social care organisations must provide information about their policies and services. Clients (in most circumstances) must be allowed access to their own notes, usually by arrangement following a written request.
Disability Discrimination Act (2005)	This requires employers and carers to take all reasonable steps to treat people with disabilities exactly the same as people without disabilities. It is just as important to respect disabled people's rights to do with information as anyone else's, even if they are unable to understand or realise you are doing this.

Legislation affecting information recording, storage and handling

Ask your manager about the arrangements in your workplace for giving a client access to their personal files.

Laws protect access to information

Reflecting the law in your working practice

The ways in which you handle information at work – the things you do, say and write – must follow the law. Individuals have the right to have their information recorded correctly, stored safely and only shared with those people who need to know – usually with that person's consent. To enable this, you should follow these guiding principles (sometimes referred to as the Caldicott Principles). You should:

- be able to justify the purpose of every item of information requested

- only share personal information if absolutely necessary

- use the minimum amount of personal information necessary to do a particular task

- access personal information on a strict need to know basis

- be aware of your responsibilities when accessing personal information

- understand and comply with the law.

Legislation Written laws, in this case governing the use of information.

Key Terms

find out!

Who has private records or confidential information about you, perhaps related to health, finance or your family? Think about why you want it kept private. What could happen if the information was recorded incorrectly? How would you feel if it was given to someone who didn't need to know it?

Be aware of your responsibilities when accessing personal information

9.2 Know where to find support for handling information and how to address difficulties

You need to know how to access guidance about the correct ways to handle, record, store, transfer and dispose of information where you work. This includes knowing where to find the policies and procedures operating within your social care organisation, as well as asking senior colleagues for advice. You also need to know how to respond appropriately if things go wrong.

Confidentiality – Places for People

We understand how difficult it is for staff to make decisions about confidential information. They worry about how to work well with other agencies (doctors, nurses, social workers in particular), friends and family of the customer while at the same time being careful not share confidential information. We also understand how easy it is for staff to make comments about customers without thinking that the information was not for sharing. We aim to make sure that all staff understand our confidentiality policy and how this works in practice. To support this we make sure that our managers encourage front line staff to ask about what they should or should not say in specific situations. Supporting staff in this way is very important.

Where do you find guidance and support about handling information?

Your workplace should have written policies and procedures relating to the way information should be handled. You should know:

🌑 where to find the policies and procedures

🌑 what they say about information handling procedures

🌑 how this affects your work role.

If the policies and procedures are very detailed or technical, ask a senior colleague to help you identify which parts are relevant for your work role. You may also learn more during staff meetings and appraisals. You should never feel reluctant to ask or check what the correct procedure for handling information is in any particular case. Your workplace should also offer training in handling information – it is important that you attend these sessions.

Case study

In Practice

Annie is a fairly new care worker in a hostel for homeless people. She reports to a senior care worker and they share a manager. She has been shown where the client paper-based files are kept and has been given a computer password so she can send emails within the organisation. Annie can also fill in assessment forms on the computer.

1. What questions does Annie need to ask, as a new employee, about information handling?

2. Where could Annie look for help and who could she ask if she has problems with information handling issues?

How do you prevent and deal with bad practice in information handling?

There are usually measures in place in social care settings to prevent bad practice in information handling. For example:

- Employees and volunteers are expected to go through a set of **vetting** procedures when beginning a job – this is known as a Criminal Records Bureau (CRB) check in England and Wales, a Protection of Vulnerable Groups (PVG) check in Scotland and a Criminal History Disclosure (CHD) in Northern Ireland.

- Staff should be properly supervised, particularly during their training period, but also afterwards.

- Agreed ways of working should be outlined in the workplace's policies and procedures, and clear rules established on reporting problems or concerns to senior managers.

- There should be physical and electronic measures in the workplace for the purpose of safely storing information.

Vetting A formal procedure to check out an individual's past record and qualifications, and particularly any police record.

Key Term

Quick Quiz

1   Which of the following is a written form of information?
    a. Telephone call
    b. Conversation with clients
    c. Multi-disciplinary team meeting
    d. Care plan

2   Why must information relating to social care clients be stored securely?
    a. To ensure it is kept neatly
    b. To protect client confidentiality
    c. To make it easy to access
    d. To make it legible

3   Which of the following forms of information should be encrypted or password protected in a social care setting?
    a. Personal files
    b. Written correspondence
    c. Electronic files
    d. Medication charts

4   Social care records can be misleading and difficult to understand if they:
    a. are written in a legible way
    b. include unexplained abbreviations
    c. are shared with other team members
    d. are not stored securely.

5   Confidentiality in relation to social care record keeping involves:
    a. keeping information about a client's health or personal circumstances secret
    b. restricting access to personal and sensitive information about clients to people who need to know
    c. being confident in the way that you write in client's records
    d. never disclosing to others information that a client gives to you 'in confidence'.

6   Jenny works in a residential care home. Darren, her supervisor, has asked Jenny to tell him her computer password so he can have a quick look at what she has written in Mrs Morgan's care records. What should Jenny do?

    a. Refuse to give Darren her password
    b. Trust Darren and give him her password
    c. Give Darren her password but stay with him until he logs off the computer
    d. Ask Darren to use his own password to access Mrs Morgan's records

7   Maria has recently developed severe depression and had her baby taken into temporary foster care. Which of the following information about her should be treated as confidential?
    a. Her mental health diagnosis
    b. The fostering of her baby
    c. Her home address
    d. All of the above

8   Confidential information relating to a social care client can be disclosed if:
    a. most members of the care team are aware of it anyway
    b. the health or safety of the client or others is at risk
    c. the information has already been discussed in a staff meeting
    d. you only reveal it to your friend or partner in confidence.

9   Which of the following laws gives social care clients the right to access their own care records?
    a. Disability Discrimination Act (2005)
    b. Human Rights Act (1998)
    c. Freedom of Information Act (2000)
    d. Data Protection Act (1998)

10 Where would a new employee in a social care team find out about information handling practices in their workplace?
    a. In the workplace policies and procedure files
    b. In their job description
    c. During their appraisal
    d. In their contract of employment

Ready for work?

REED
SOCIAL CARE

Throughout this course you have been furnished with the tools to successfully apply for positions within the adult social care sector.

What follows is a checklist of things you should have done during the course to ensure that you are well placed to successfully apply and interview for the positions which interest you.

Checklist

☑ **CV** – produce a concise, well presented CV that complies with data confidentiality (see reed.co.uk for advice).

☑ Work experience – try to obtain some voluntary work experience to strengthen your application. Speak to local organisations to see if you can work with them.

☑ **Research** – make a list of local companies that you feel you would like to work for and find out what they do. Researching these companies at this stage will make applying to work for them later much easier. It will also help a recruitment agency find a suitable position for you if you have a good understanding of the types of organisation you would like to work for.

☑ **Extra activities** – think about extra activities that you have done or could do to strengthen your CV by demonstrating leadership skills, inspiration and improvement.

☑ **Weaknesses** – think about any areas in your skills and experience that you feel could be improved. These are essential for interview, and you should also think about ways to improve them.

☑ **Interview practice** – practise interview questions with your friends or family, to improve your confidence when you attend the real thing. Look online at reed.co.uk for tips on interview questions, and example questions that you might be asked.

☑ **Personal Development Plan (PDP)** – create a PDP, detailing your training experience and courses that you would like to take in the future. This will help you to have a clear idea about where you would like your career to go. This kind of information can also be helpful to any recruitment agency that you may choose to visit.

☑ **References** – these are essential if you want to work in the social care sector. As you come to the end of any voluntary work, make sure you obtain the details of somebody you can ask for a reference when applying for future jobs. Also, keep track of people from your time in education – if you do not have much professional experience, educational references will be important. You should keep a list of these references in your work pack – they will be asked for by both recruitment agencies and any prospective employers that you apply to work for.

Applying for jobs

Now that you have successfully created your CV using advice from reed.co.uk, you are ready to start applying for jobs. The following checklist gives a number of steps that you should take to ensure that you have the best chance of finding the job you want.

Checklist

☑ **Set up email alerts** – use reed.co.uk to set up an email alert which will come through to you when new jobs are posted in the social care sector. This will enable you to apply quickly when new jobs are posted, as well as keeping you aware of opportunities in the market.

☑ **Apply for jobs online** – using reed.co.uk, search for positions in the social care sector that are near where you live. If you find something that interests you, then apply! Write a brief covering letter to accompany your CV – make sure that it makes specific reference to the position that you are applying for, but don't make it too long.

☑ **Register with your local Reed Social Care branch** – phone or visit them to make an appointment to do this. When meeting a consultant, ensure that you take along all the documentation that you have been asked to bring – you won't be able to register without it. Registering with a Reed consultant means that you increase your chances of finding the right job for you. You should be honest about your skills and experience, as that will aid the consultant in matching you to jobs that would interest and benefit you. Reed Social Care has a variety of temporary and permanent positions available throughout the UK.

Glossary

Abbreviations Shortened forms of words or phrases; for example, 'meds' for 'medicines', or ENT for 'Ear, Nose and Throat'.

Accountable Answerable to someone or responsible for some action.

Acronym A word formed by the first letters of other words, for example GP (general practitioner).

Adult at risk Anyone aged 18 years and over who might not be able to protect themselves because they are ill, disabled or older.

Assistive technologies Technological solutions that support telehealth, telecare and telemedicine. Examples are blood pressure and blood glucose monitoring machines sending the results by telephone to a healthcare professional, and using email and or Skype to communicate with individuals, perhaps on a more regular basis than would otherwise be possible.

Attachment relationship A relationship that is based on strong emotional bonds.

Braille A system widely used by blind people to read and write. Each character consists of up to six raised dots arranged in a rectangle.

Capacity The mental or physical ability to do something.

Code of Practice A set of guidelines and expectations that must be followed.

Coerce Force someone to do something against their will.

Collude Co-operate with somebody in order to do something illegal or to keep it secret.

Commission Deliberately doing something while knowing the consequences.

Confidential information Information that may only be accessed by individuals who have the authority or permission to access it.

Confidentiality The process of recognising certain information as sensitive, keeping it secure and only sharing it with those who need to know in order to provide care and support.

Consent Giving informed agreement to or permission for something to happen, such as an action or decision. Establishing consent varies according to individual's assessed capacity to give consent.

Contagious A disease that is spread by physical contact.

Core temperature The temperature of the thickest part of the meat; for example, in between the breast and leg of a whole chicken.

Cystic fibrosis An inherited disease affecting the lungs and digestive system. The body produces abnormal sticky mucous resulting in chronic respiratory infections and impaired pancreatic function.

Dementia A condition affecting the brain. People with dementia often have memory problems and there may be changes in the way the person experiences their surroundings; they will need extra support with communication.

Dignity Having respect and status. It is generally accepted that everyone has the right to dignity and ethical treatment. Dignity is closely linked to human rights.

Direct discrimination When a person is treated less well than someone else because of a protected characteristic (what makes them different).

Diversity The value of our differences.

Effective communication Sharing meaningful information between two or more people; the goal is that the receiver understands the sender's intended message.

Emotional intelligence Includes self-awareness, impulse control, motivation and empathy – some of the qualities that underpin the outstanding communication skills in those people who have successful relationships at home and work.

Empathy The ability to understand and share someone else's feelings or situation.

Empowerment Gaining more control over your life by having opportunities to develop greater self-confidence and self-esteem.

Encrypted files Electronic files protected by a code that is protected by a password.

Ergonomics Fitting a task to the individual, their capabilities, strength, stability and mental capacity. It can involve the use of aids.

Establishing consent The process of establishing informed agreement to an action or decision with individuals, while ensuring that individuals have access to the appropriate information.

Formal relationship A relationship that is based on agreed, formal rules between employers and employees and with colleagues in a workplace.

Hazard A hazard is an actual threat to one's health or something that could cause an accident such as a spillage of grease where someone will be walking.

Indirect discrimination When a rule or way of doing things is put in place that has a worse impact on someone with a protected characteristic (because they are different) than someone without one; and cannot be justified.

Induction Introduction to a new work role, including orientation and training.

Informed consent Permission given in full knowledge of the possible consequences (risks and benefits).

Job description A written statement that describes the duties and responsibilities of a job.

Legible Describes writing that is easy to read, especially handwriting.

Legislation Written laws, in this case governing the use of information.

Life Story Network Life Story Network is particularly useful for people with memory difficulties such as dementia, and for people who are depressed or withdrawn.

Local Government Ombudsman Independent authority that investigates unresolved or complex complaints.

Makaton A system of signs and symbols to help communication. It supports the spoken word by using the signs and symbols in spoken word order.

Mental capacity Ability to comprehend; to understand, The Mental Capacity Act 2005 gives a legal definition of 'mental capacity' and aims to protect people who are not able to make their own decisions.

Moral Describes behaving in a way that is good and appropriate.

Multi-agency working An arrangement where workers from different agencies or organisations work together.

Multi-disciplinary working This is where different care professionals work together in the same team.

Negligence Conduct that falls below the accepted standard of behaviour, resulting in an unreasonable risk of harm.

Norm Accepted, normal behaviour.

Ofsted 'Office for Standards in Education Children's services and skills'. Ofsted's role is to inspect and regulate all services for children and young people.

Omission Where something is either deliberately or accidentally not done.

Pathogenic bacteria Harmful bacteria that can make people ill if transmitted.

Plain English Communication styles that are clear, brief and to the point and avoid technical language, particularly in relation to official communication.

Positive risk taking Taking risks in a deliberate and purposeful way. Sometimes people choose to take risks to improve their quality of life.

PPE The acronym for 'Personal Protective Equipment'. It is anything that creates a barrier between the worker and possible contamination. Examples are disposable gloves and aprons, caps, nets or hats for food handlers.

'Protected characteristics' In the Equality Act as it applies to users of a service are age, disability, gender reassignment, marriage and civil partnership, pregnancy and maternity, race, religion or belief, sex, sexual orientation.

Re-ablement Describes the idea of 'making possible again' rather than restoring previous function. It is a little different from rehabilitation because it involves understanding the whole person rather than just what is physically 'wrong'.

Retribution Something done to injure, punish or 'get back' at someone.

Risk The possibility of something potentially hazardous such as an open window near a wasp's nest where a wasp may enter through the window and sting someone.

Risk assessment The process of identifying and estimating the levels of risk, comparing this against standards and agreeing an acceptable level of risk.

Risk taking Enabling and supporting the person to make informed choices and decisions by understanding and taking responsibility for their actions and the consequences.

Safeguarding Ensuring the individual is safe from abuse and neglect, and helping people to make choices independently.

Self-esteem Your belief about your self-worth.

Sign language Uses visual sign patterns to convey meaning by combining hand shapes, and movement of the hands, arms or body, and facial expressions. British Sign Language (BSL) is the preferred sign language in the UK.

Socialisation The way in which a person learns about the world around them, and the values and expectations of the society they live in.

Standard procedures Approved ways of working to be followed as a routine.

Stressor Anything that can trigger feelings of being unable to cope, being under stress or under pressure.

Stroke A stroke is caused by a blockage in a blood vessel or a bleed into the brain. This damages part of the brain and the function associated with that part. Strokes affect people in different ways, depending on the part of the brain that is affected and the extent of the damage. Recovery from a stroke depends partly on the speed at which the condition is recognised and first treatment is given.

Unsafe practice An approach or standard of care that puts individuals at risk.

Verbal communication When a message is delivered by being spoken.

Vetting A formal procedure to check out an individual's past record and qualifications, and particularly any police record.

Vulnerable More likely to suffer risk and harm.

Well-being Factors such as biological, health, spiritual, emotional, cultural, religious and social satisfaction come together to create a person's well-being.

Whistle blowing Exposing poor practice to try to stop it from happening.

Index